More Praise & Personal Success Stories for Yvonne Oswald's *Every Word Has Power*

"In *Every Word Has Power*, Yvonne Oswald tells us, 'true success is when you feel great about who you are, what you do, and what you have.' This book can help you get there."

Ric Giardina, author of *Becoming a Life Balance Master*, creative director of The Spirit Employed Company

"Master your spoken words and you direct your life. Master your internal thoughts and you direct your destiny! Take your success to the next level with *Every Word Has Power*. Yvonne answers questions you didn't even know you had to ask!"

Marcia Martin, BSc, Power Speaking Seminars, transformational trainer

Yvonne Oswald, winner of 2007's "Most Unique Contribution to the field of Hypnotherapy and Personal Growth," awarded by the Association of Transpersonal Hypnotherapists

"*Every Word Has Power* is a must read for anyone that is working with the Law of Attraction. It truly is THE handbook to teach you how to apply the laws in order to create what you desire. It provides easy, simple, and practical ways to raise your vibration. I will recommend it to all my clients!"

Christy Whitman, bestselling author, professional speaker, and certified Law of Attraction coach

"Changing my words consciously has changed my whole attitude and that of my clients. I have seen miraculous results in depression and amazing, healing results from inviting clients to 'switch' their words. The significant changes that I observe daily in my practice is that I achieve results far more quickly, and people appear to be so much more optimistic."

Dr. Ebi Taebi, doctor of naturopathic medicine and specialist in cancer, chronic disease, and depression

"Yvonne Oswald is a brilliant teacher and healer. I highly recommend this book . . . a truly transformative read."

Colette Baron-Reid, bestselling author of
Remembering the Future: The Path to Recovering Intuition

"Being aware of my language has transformed my life in unexpected ways. It has shown me where I need to heal. I learned that any unpleasant thought I had came with a corresponding unpleasant feeling. As I consciously began to change my thoughts, my feelings towards my husband grew more loving and accepting. It felt like my heart was expanding, and I saw him through compassionate eyes. Our interactions became more positive because he was open to using the same tools. Happily, we have fallen in love all over again."

Dr. Carrie Bailey, PhD, psychologist, Connect Department, Canadian Hearing Society

"Transforming words such as 'problem' and 'bad' into opportunity . . . has helped me transform my speech and my way of thinking! Thank you, Yvonne! By becoming aware of my own language patterns and changing them, I am finding life so much more easy, and my prosperity has increased to the point where I recently put a deposit on a condo, which I am already well on the way to being able to buy with cash by the time it is built."

Elaine Charal, graphologist and handwriting analyst

"This book showed me in very basic and easy-to-understand terms how my own internal and external language patterns were actually creating my life. The first step to my successful life transformation was becoming aware of how often I chose nonsupportive words in my day-to-day speech. With practice and patience, this simple, positive shift in my vocabulary greatly improved my family life—with my children and my husband— as well as shifted my gears into high for my business relationships and sales."

Rose-Anne Kumpunen, owner of *www.RealLifeChanges.com*

"I thought I was a very positive person until I read [Yvonne's] book and realized how much my negative thought patterns were affecting every aspect of my day-to-day living. Change is not easy, but thanks to this book, I now have tools to bring about a more positive and beneficial change to my life. I've bought a copy of the book for all of my friends and relatives! Thank you, Yvonne."

Ann Singer, market researcher

"Things were not going well between me and a colleague— so much so that I was starting to make myself physically ill . . . from all the emotion. We needed to have a conversation. Just when things were at their darkest, I remembered that focusing on the negative was causing me to get more of the same. As soon as I harnessed the power of the unconscious and switched my self-talk, the situation turned around. Using high-vibration words allowed me to have a productive dialogue and both of us to come away as winners."

Carol-Ann Hamilton, corporate trainer and life coach

Every Word Has Power

Every Word Has Power

SWITCH ON YOUR LANGUAGE AND TURN ON YOUR LIFE

Yvonne Oswald
MHT, MNLP, MTLT™

ATRIA BOOKS
New York London Toronto Sydney

ATRIA BOOKS
A Division of Simon & Schuster, Inc.
1230 Avenue of the Americas
New York, NY 10020

20827 N.W. Cornell Road, Suite 500
Hillsboro, Oregon 97124–9808

Managing editor: Lindsay S. Brown
Editor: Julie Clayton
Copyeditor: Meadowlark Communications, Inc.
Proofreader: Jennifer Weaver-Neist
Cover/interior design: Sara E. Blum
Composition: William H. Brunson Typography Services

First Atria Books/Beyond Words hardcover edition March 2008

ATRIA BOOKS and colophon are trademarks of Simon & Schuster, Inc.
Beyond Words Publishing is a division of Simon & Schuster, Inc.

Manufactured in the United States of America

ISBN-13: 978-1-58270-181-3

With Special Thanks

This book is dedicated with love and gratitude to the two loves of my life—Will, my husband, and Katie, my daughter—for their total support and inspiration.

Special thanks to:

Cynthia Black and Richard Cohn, my publishers, for their vision and for believing in me; Julie Clayton, my editor, for her amazing empathy and abilities; Lane Pierce for his warmth and generosity; Robert Doyle, for his brilliant mind and perceptions; and Carrie Bailey and Colette Baron-Reid, who have my admiration for their passion for life.

My family:

Mother Ruth and sisters Jen, Val, Treena, and Ann for being there for me.

Blessings to:

Elaine Charal and Sheena Gaidy for their years of loyalty and assistance, and to you, the lightworker who is with me on the path.

Contents

Appendix

Preface

Your Words Will Set You Free

The very words you speak and think are your personal vehicle on your journey to happiness. They program both your destination and the speed with which you get there. Words change your DNA sequences by recreating your future and creating quantum possibilities that allow you to take control of your destiny. Words and thoughts shape your very character. Take your place in the sun and learn to design your life intentionally NOW.

Introduction

The Power of Words

How would you like to be able to clear negative emotions and limiting beliefs to make space for success in less than a minute?

How would you like to be able to access high-energy states to open up vast internal resources and connect with an abundant universe?

How would you like to increase your dialogue with others and your internal self-talk to the extent that you get all of your needs met easily and efficiently?

All of this and more is possible when we enter the uncharted realms of our very own minds.

A study by Raymond Birdwhistle in 1970 proved that the words you speak to others represent just *7 percent* of the results you get from your communication. The words you speak to yourself, however, generate *100 percent* of the results you'll get in your life, as your own amazing mind interprets and follows your instructions.

You are already a Master Communicator. How well you communicate depends entirely on the response you get, which means that you alone are responsible for how the other person understands you. In fact, your success in every area of your life depends on your ability to make yourself understood.

The nine chapters that follow are profoundly simple yet metamorphic and will show you how to "switch on" your language, leading you to a wonderful destiny that is full of rewards: better communication, better relationships, improved well-being, achieving your innermost desires, and making your dreams come true. You will also learn the difference between low-energy and high-energy words and how they affect your life. All the knowledge, love, success, prosperity, health, and happiness that you deserve are already yours, just waiting for you to use the correct words to connect with them.

Let's explore a little background information before we start.

Where Did Communication Begin?

The use of gestures and body language predates spoken language. Many researchers believe this form of communicating began at least four million years ago, when *bipedalism*, a characteristic of the hominid line, freed up the hands and enabled "expressive" communication.

Evidence of groups and socialization also appeared around this time, and nonverbal communication emerged—waving, gesturing, and so on—which may have evolved as a result of the more cohesive and cooperative social structures that were emerging. One of the benefits of nonverbal communication is its silent nature, a great protective device around predators. Intentional nonverbal communication, such as pointing (an indication of spatial awareness), is not found in other primates and is the one thing that separates us from other species.

In fact, according to a study done at the Max Planck Institute in 1997, human babies point automatically several weeks before spoken words emerge.

The brain has three major parts: the reptilian brain, the middle or limbic brain, and the cerebral cortex, the most recently developed part of the brain. The ancient reptilian brain's focus is physical movement and survival. The middle brain links mainly with our emotions: fear, anger, love, affection, and communication. It's called the family, or limbic brain. This is the group brain system that started to evolve as we began to socialize. Its goals are short-term and focus primarily on good/bad, right/wrong, and yours/mine. It's habitual, hierarchical, and simplistic. It does not have a capacity to visualize or grow because it thinks in terms of *polarities*. The newest part of the brain is the cerebral cortex. "New" is relative, of course! It only developed in the last hundred and fifty to two hundred thousand years, and it is here that language began, in the form of gestures.

When we speak today, we still use gestures and body language to supplement our communication. In fact, we unconsciously use body language for 55 percent of all communication. Just ask someone to describe what a spiral looks like using only words!

Complex language as we know it only emerged around sixty-five thousand years ago. Its origin could explain why *Homo sapiens* came to dominate both the Neanderthals of Europe and *Homo erectus* of Southeast Asia, because the amazing property of speech that makes it different from any other form of communication is its ability to be *generative*. Tribes developing complex speech were able to imagine a future, and hence create a place for themselves in it. We can now think back into the past and forward into the future with elegance and speed. We can fantasize and imagine beyond and outside space and time, giving us infinite possibilities that can be conveyed with just a single word!

However, the language that we use now still has words that were formulated sixty-five thousand years ago to describe the feelings and emotions that were emerging from the middle brain's polarity thinking. If we consciously change our language—the words we use in talking to ourselves and others—then we update our neural patterns to reflect our more sophisticated faculties, and consciously create a different, more open, and happier world for ourselves.

Essential to language is the ability to understand and take on the mental perspective of others. "Mirror" neurons are active when a monkey or human is watching someone's actions: quite possibly the neural beginnings of establishing "rapport," which I will teach you how to use in detail later in the book. To date, apart from primates, the only other species we know of that have and use mirror neurons are elephants, dolphins, and parrots.

Open the Magic Inside Your Mind

The neocortex (Latin for "new bark" or "new rind") forms the top layer of the cerebral cortex and is the most recent part of the brain to develop. Neocortical inputs are mainly from the frontal lobe, which modulates initiative, imagination, and social awareness. This higher brain function is where your magic formula for happiness begins as you connect with the higher consciousness. Use of the higher brain produces consistent success in your everyday life. You can now plan your goals and visualize wonderful possibilities with this magical tool. Rather than use the higher brain to rescue yourself when you feel less than happy, it's time to learn to utilize it and live in it by "spring cleaning" your language of antiquated middle-brain polarity thought processes—going beyond what you ever thought possible to achieve.

In chapter five you will learn how to clear the interference patterns of past low-energy emotions and nonsupportive beliefs, so that you can increase your ability to manifest your desires by directly accessing the higher brain. The creative integration of the recently developed cerebral cortex with the older limbic brain allows you to tap into the whole system.

By clearing interference patterns from your mind, you encourage the higher consciousness in the cerebral cortex to develop. You gain clarity. You experience a continuous sense of inner peace and trust, even when things are not going as well as you'd like.

In fact, things will move through your life much more quickly as you leap to higher levels of consciousness. You find, then, that you are always in a state of confidence, feeling empowered, in control, and self-motivated. You can come into your full power as a person. You love who and where you are in your life, and you are hopeful for the progress of humanity. As your trust levels increase, so does your motivation to help other people to be successful.

Using the tools and knowledge offered in this book, you can now connect in a nanosecond to a vast reservoir of previously untapped knowledge and power by clearing low-energy words from your thoughts and language, and switching to high-energy words.

Low-energy words accompany low-energy thoughts and emotions—usually these are unconscious (meaning that we are unaware of them) beliefs and models we hold for ourselves and the world that are less than supportive and keep us from being as successful

Introduction

as we would like to be. Most of us have some degree of low-energy self-talk, such as "I'm not good enough" or "I don't deserve to be happy/rich," and this low energy spills over into our communication with others. It also acts like static interference internally so that goals and desires might seem less easy to achieve.

High-energy words accompany high-energy thoughts, and unlike low-energy words, we can practice using high-energy words until our thoughts and emotions adjust in kind. Then our life becomes quite simply and profoundly a positive, high-energy experience, with minimal stretch required.

The combination of learning to switch our internal and external dialogue and removing limiting beliefs and negative (low-energy) emotions sends the mind clear and intentional signals that beam rewards directly back to us. When we do this, we create a direct connection to the quantum power of the universal consciousness that we call God, or the Universal Mind: the pure consciousness beyond our known parameters.

How would you feel if you had the ability to clear any negative emotion from the low moments of your life in less than a minute, and could remember them with the same feelings of satisfaction as the high moments? How much better will your life be when I teach you how to consciously use high-energy words? How would you like to learn Magic of the Mind—techniques and exercises for instantly changing your emotional state or mental disposition?

This book offers elegantly easy exercises that help you to transition smoothly into taking charge of your own life. The enhanced knowledge that you are about to discover has the capacity to take you to a new frontier of human behavioral technology.

For over twenty years I have been enriching people's lives as a therapist and facilitator, practicing and teaching others how to enhance and transform their personal lives and careers through the power of words. Here I use the knowledge I've gained from counseling and consulting with thousands of people from all walks of life so that you, too, can discover the specific ways you can direct your destiny.

You'll learn a new, easy approach to making decisions and will develop, grow, and awaken all of your positive potential. You'll learn to value who you are and transform your self-image. You'll find new ways to increase self-confidence and release negative emotions and limiting beliefs, opening you to the bounteous abundance and prosperity that is simply waiting to be claimed. In close relationships, you'll learn to be more willing to accept deeper emotional commitment, and find a new level of trust and openness in all of your encounters with others. You'll stretch to take advantage of new opportunities once you know that you can accomplish anything you put your mind to. You'll gain momentum and make real progress as you learn to direct your passion and energy in fun, inspiring ways with fast and tangible results. To take advantage of all the great tools in this book, you may want to start by having a notebook and pen ready to take notes and do the easy exercises as you go through each chapter.

Are you ready right now to switch on your word power? Then join me on a pioneering and inspiring journey. Come and learn to speak and think your wonderful future into reality, one word and one thought at a time.

Give life to your words, and your words will bring life, love, and success to YOU.

1

The Power of
Clear Decisions

Be present to life, because life is a present.

Choice and Change Bring Freedom

You can change your mind with the speed of thought. Your unconscious mind is capable of making changes faster than you ever imagined possible. The truth is that "reality" is simply your perception of what you believe to be true. Yesterday you believed that today was tomorrow. Tomorrow you'll believe that today was yesterday. When you were six you believed you were six. You had a birthday and the next day you believed you were seven. You see, hear, feel, think, and believe simply what you focus on. You have the knowledge and wisdom of eternity in every cell of your body.

Decision-making is all about correcting outdated thoughts and ... changing your mind. It's your conscious mind that makes choices and decisions. Inner change happens at the unconscious level and is instantaneous. You might hear people say that it took them a year to give up smoking. It might have taken a year to make the *decision* to change the habit; however, it took less than a second to actually stop.

Many people tell me that they don't find it easy to make decisions. Let's just consider this: if you are awake for sixteen or seventeen hours a day and you make just one choice every minute (what to eat, what to think, what to say, how to breathe, what body movements you can make, which exercise to do, where to go next, who to talk to), you consciously make at least one thousand decisions every single day. So, we've just established that you already know how to make up your mind on a regular basis. How do you arrive at conclusions about more substantial decisions?

Let me show you how simple it can be. Are you ready with your notebook to track your progress toward a brighter future?

Easy Decision-Making: One-to-Ten

Decision-making using One-to-Ten is a form of applied kinesiology. Kinesiology is a method of testing the muscle response stimulus in the body, and has been well established and corroborated scientifically now for more than twenty years. From the original research of Dr. George Goodheart, Dr. John Diamond studied and demonstrated the fact that muscles respond to both physical and mental stimuli. Your mind/body connection has such a powerful survival mechanism that your muscles react instantly to truths and nontruths, to what is good for you and what is not good for you. This is a fast, easy, and reliable method that will foster in you trust in your own judgment, helping you to make rapid and confident decisions. Your sensory awareness will increase exponentially the more you use it, allowing you to calibrate your life on a day-by-day basis. You can rethink your future strategies using this new tool.

Two months after the birth of my daughter Katie I was extremely hormonal and not functioning well. I went from being an extremely capable woman to a person who could barely manage day-to-day tasks. Sometimes, not even those.

One day my husband Will asked me to look up a phone number and my reply was, "I can't do that today." I really meant it. My day was mapped out in tiny steps to allow me to cope, and finding a phone number appeared to be a huge task. Decision-making was even more interesting. I found I could not prioritize. The day I discovered my One-to-Ten method, I hired a babysitter for the first time, to have a two-hour respite from mothering. I couldn't make up my mind whether to go shopping or swimming. Twenty minutes went by and I was still sitting on the couch asking myself, "Shopping or swimming? Shopping or swimming?"

Finally, I snapped out of it by thinking, "Alright, Yvonne. Give me a number between one and ten (one being low and ten being high): which would do me more good, shopping or swimming?" The answer: "Swimming—seven; shopping—four. Okay, swimming it is!" That swim was one of the best of my life.

I started applying the method to simple decisions, such as what I would have for breakfast: "Toast—seven; cereal—two. Toast it is." I found that this approach worked for everything, so much so that I was then able to apply it to more important decisions.

The inner you, your unconscious mind, which is where these answers come from, "knows" much better than your conscious mind the state of the universe as it applies to your needs (not desires), because it has your best interests at heart. It, along with every one of the fifty to one hundred trillion cells in your body, is eagerly listening to your instructions right this moment.

You can test the method to find out how much you are in touch with the inner you by simply stating a true or untrue statement and asking yourself what number between one and ten comes up. So, for me: "My name is Jim: zero out of ten. My name is Yvonne: ten out of ten."

Do the One-to-Ten decision-making with simple daily decisions at first, such as "How good is it for me to have pasta tonight?" The more quickly you can come up with the answer, the more you can trust it. The one thing to remember is this: *If the number you come up with is five or below, the answer is NO.*

"How good is it for me to . . . ?" is a far better question to ask than "Do I *want* to . . . ?" Yes, you may want to marry Jim (or Mary), but would it be *good* for you? That might be an entirely different matter. *How* you ask is extremely important for clear decision-making.

By asking "How good is Jim for me at the moment?" you may come up with a seven, which means that he is either teaching you a larger lesson of some kind (even if that lesson isn't making you happy), or that he is really good for you right now. By asking, "How good will Jim be for me in five years time?" your response may go down to a four, which means that it is not a matter of *if* but *when* the relationship will end, so it's not leading anywhere. Check out all your friendships with this method. You may get some interesting results.

Ask yourself this one: "How good is my job for me right now?" If your answer is five or below, start looking elsewhere for another one because you're already past the leaving date!

Don't trust your intuition yet? Use this method every day for a month for small things, such as "What does my body *need* for lunch?"

Another way to begin the question is to ask, "How likely is it that ...?" I find this phrase very useful for financial decisions. For example, "How likely am I to make money from this new venture?"

"How good is it ..." can also be modified: "How good is this career change for me financially/emotionally/physically/mentally?" Sometimes you may come up with answers of two and eight at the same time. If that happens, reverse the question: "How good is it for me to take a holiday?" Answer: two and eight (two because perhaps you are too busy right now to enjoy a trip and eight because you really need a break!). "How good is it for me *not* to take a holiday?" Answer: two out of ten. Plan the holiday for the end of your busy time and enjoy the trip! The reason that your mind overrides the "not" element of this sentence is that the significant negative burst of energy produced by the thought of staying and working versus taking a holiday makes the unconscious mind search for a healthy alternative. It is the unconscious mind's prime directive to keep us alive and healthy, and it will leap at any opportunity to do so.

Have fun learning to trust your innate decision-making ability. After just one week you'll be much more in touch with what your body, mind, and spirit need to stay balanced, and your natural instincts will be improved.

Are We There Yet?

Now that you know how to make decisions more easily, what exactly can you change to "switch on" your life? Anything and everything that is not working well for you can be changed. You have all of the answers inside your mind. You have a solution to every one of your questions because your inner mind is programmed to search for wholeness and well-being. So, what exactly do you need to make you happy and free?

Many years ago, when I began to counsel people, I used to feel that there were hundreds of queries about life's choices. I took the time one day and actually wrote them down on paper. I was surprised by how few there really are. This is the list I compiled: Birth; Career; Creativity; Death; Family (parents, children, siblings, children); Fun; Health (physical, mental, emotional, spiritual); Home; Life's purpose(s); Money; Relationships (partner/spouse, friends, colleagues); Self-image; Self-growth; and Travel.

There are not many more than that. What I realized, though, is that many of these life choices require no actual change, even when they don't meet our desires. They simply require further knowledge or a change of perspective. We cannot, for instance, change our family. We can only change ourselves and our reaction to our family.

What we *can* change most easily will switch us to balance, harmony, and self-empowerment, igniting passion and resulting in a life of joy and accomplishment. Flexibility—the ability to choose how we respond to our life events—opens up the most choices for clear decision-making.

Before you can begin to set goals for yourself, make fundamental changes, and open up your future, it's useful to know how balanced your life is right now. To determine this, use the table on the following page. In the first column, based on how great and happy you feel, rate your satisfaction level for each area of your life from 0 to 100 percent. You may want to expand some of the categories such as I have done under "Relationships." For instance, "Money" can be divided into investments and earned income.

If you wrote down 80 percent or more in each key area of your life in the Great/Happy column, this is ideal. If this were a

Snapshot of Your Happiness Rating

Key Area	% of Great/ Happy (0–100%)	Easiest Area to Make Changes (check)	Specific Action (within twenty-four hours)
Health: Physical	70		
Mental	80		
Emotional	60		
Spiritual	80		
Self-Worth	70		
Relationships: Partner/spouse	40		
Family	50		
Friends	40		
Fun	90		
Creativity	60		
Learning	70		
Money	40 50		
Career	50		
Home	90		
Overall Happiness	80		

business balance sheet, 50 percent would mean that you were working a lot for no profit! Less than 50 percent simply means that immediate attention is required—not action, necessarily, but attention. Normally you would tend to try to activate this low-percentage key area, as it would be the one that's metaphorically jumping up and down, demanding the most limelight.

However, think about what happens when you focus on trying (yes, I used that word intentionally) to remember someone's name that's on the tip of your tongue. As soon as you divert your attention elsewhere, your unconscious mind is free to go away and retrieve the information, and the name just pops into your mind easily. So, for the time being, just observe the lowest-energy area simply with interest and without focus or action.

Next, working further with your answers in the first column, I'd like you to circle the key areas less than 50 percent. Usually if one of the key areas is less than 50 percent, then fun and creativity are also low, because great imbalance tends to manifest negative emotions as your mind attempts to send you a message to take charge of your life.

In the next column, check two or three areas that you can most *easily* act on immediately. Of the areas you checked, write down one small thing in the last column that you can do within twenty-four hours to start creating movement. For instance, if money is not great right now, you might call a friend and go out (as long as it doesn't cost much). Or you might go for a walk or read a good book. If your relationship is in the lower percentage, you might organize a date night or give your partner a compliment. Go bowling or dancing. Physical activity stimulates change at the quantum level and will activate endorphins to make you feel good. You are, in effect, rewarding yourself. There's a list of rewards in chapter two to give you some other ideas.

If you're still not sure where to start, "fun" is the easiest area to initiate. Your primary goal is immediacy. The more quickly you start making changes, the sooner you'll feel better. A small change in any one area of your life will have a chain reaction and initiate change in all the other areas. Commit to doing something now; go ahead and begin to switch on your life.

If you want to activate a particular area of your life right now but circumstances do not allow immediate action, then all you can change is your perception of it or your belief about it. Ask yourself what positive lesson you can take from the circumstance and then make a decision to review it at a specific date—say, six, eight, or twelve months ahead. Actually write or type the date into your day planner and then let it go. Now you can pay full attention instead to what you *can* change easily. What normally happens is that as you change other aspects of your life, opening up new options, the situation that appeared to have the least possibility of movement suddenly gets much more flexible.

As you change your inner talk, become more self-aware, and make new decisions, you'll find yourself more easily able to adapt and adjust quickly. Your health will improve because intuition, optimism, and action become a natural, everyday part of your life. True, vital health and peak performance happen when you are balanced on every level: physical, mental, emotional, and spiritual. It's through your self-talk and imagination that you can direct yourself to a dynamic life. Your reality can be as good as your heart desires because, if you can imagine it, your unconscious believes it to be true and can attract it for you.

Inner Resources

Your whole body is an energy-sensing device. You are, in effect, like a radio that can receive hundreds of stations. Many people go through life thinking that they are simply a receiving station, without realizing that they are also a broadcasting station, able to amplify energy and change the future. Fast-forwarding your life can be as easy as turning the dial or pushing a button! That means taking action to target what you want as you clear out the static of negative words, low energy emotions, or limiting beliefs, and awakening the untapped energy inside your mind to take you to a life of empowerment.

Real empowerment is about calling on your inner resources and strengths in challenging times. Each new experience develops and activates the innate, latent forces inside you; the more resources you construct, the more resilient you become. You may still have an occasional day when you don't feel great, but you'll bounce back much more quickly, and be, do, and have even better than before as you discover new and supportive strategies. You'll learn to trust your inner mind to find out what's working and what isn't as you reformulate and re-map to build momentum.

Your success rate and growth are dependent on your ability to recognize, define, process, predict, and direct information toward

a specific goal. The choices and decisions you mak[e]
your knowledge, beliefs, and feelings, which are dra[wn]
previous results or memories. Your memories influe[nce]
view and influence other people. They also create y[our]
they are your primary resource center.

James McGaugh, a neurobiologist at the University of California, Irvine, says that everything you do as a human being is based
on your memories: all of your aspirations, your experiences, and
your abilities to communicate. He explains that your beliefs about
yourself are based on your memories and that memories are
essential to life.

The process—and it *is* a process—begins with paying particular
attention to your thoughts. It begins with changing every word
you speak so that your thoughts, language, and intent become
crystal clear. It's like human mind nanotechnology.

Happy Changing

*What you perceive is what you believe. How you perceive is what
you'll achieve.*

Your inner (unconscious) mind loves to learn and integrate
new ideas, finding solutions to erase and transform old patterns
into new, dynamic action that brings you forward into joy. You
are about to learn how to accept and let go consciously what cannot be changed, and change what *can* be changed as soon as you
become aware that something is not working out well. This will
help you to make clear decisions that are truly based on what sup-
ports you.

Your thoughts start out as observations, ideas, or symbols and
are translated by your conscious mind into words. Words are simply a physical, measurable manifestation of these thoughts. They
are your way of making sense of what you perceive. The words
you think or say then form a picture, feeling, or symbol in your
unconscious mind (the "language" of the unconscious mind is
nonverbal), which goes off to search for and bring you whatever
you focus on. It also stores and retrieves every chain of meaning

ciated with every single word you utter and every thought you think. So, the words you use to communicate with your unconscious mind (and therefore yourself) are bringing you either high-energy results or low-energy results, depending on the feeling or symbol underlying the high-energy or low-energy words you use.

Positive Words, Positive Decisions

What motivates us to be happy, rich, or healthy? Do you think about getting out of debt, or do you think about making money? Do you look after your health only when you become unwell, or do you take care of your health all the time? Do you nurture your relationship, or do you stay in a less than happy relationship because you are "comfortable"?

I was doing a therapy session on prosperity with Karen. I always ask a very simple question at the beginning of a private session: "Why are you here today?" It's amazing how many times that question produces a response that is not at all what the person had initially said they wanted to change.

Karen replied, "Because I'm sick of being in *debt*."

"Why else are you here?"

"Because I don't want to be *poor*."

"Why else are you here?"

"Because I don't want to *end up on the streets sick and poor* when I'm an old lady. I want a *better life*."

At last I had something positive to work with!

"So, what will you be doing when you have a better life?"

"I'll be living *stress-free*. I won't be *poor* any more."

If you study the key words Karen used in her speech, and therefore the key words in her thought patterns, you can see that her words were concentrated on what she *didn't* want, and it took some encouragement to shift them toward what she *did* want. Unconsciously then, through her language, Karen was directing her inner mind to seek and increase her state of debt and anxiety. No wonder she was not attracting prosperity.

Change Your Words, Change Your World

Do you remember every good thing that ever happened to you? Your unconscious mind does, and will remind you of every good incident simply by your focusing your attention on the word *good*. You'll feel better without even knowing why. The reason for this is that each key word has its own individual frequency. Powerful, high-energy words such as *excitement, joy, success,* or *love,* vibrate higher and faster, thus increasing your "I feel good" feelings.

Low-energy words, particularly words that have a negative emotional association such as *sadness* or *guilt,* resonate at a lower frequency. They make you feel less than great by literally lowering your energy levels. In fact, 20 percent of the words you use have strong emotional undertones, which cause you to react either negatively or positively.

Did you know that *being happy adds nine years to your life*? It has been scientifically proven that low-energy thoughts lower the immune system and make people more illness-prone. In a BBC News study published in 2003, researchers from the University of Wisconsin measured the electrical brain activity of fifty people between the ages of fifty-seven and sixty. Those with the highest levels of activity in the right prefrontal cortex (the pessimists) hardly reacted to a flu vaccine. Those with the strongest activity in the left prefrontal cortex (the happy thoughts people) had much stronger immune systems and produced many more antibodies in response to the vaccine.

Doing an Internet search on the word "good" brought up more than a billion websites. When I typed in "bad" I found half that many. Inside your mind, those websites represent all the memories (this life, genetic, and even past-life) and chains of meaning associated with the words. This means that by focusing your language on the word *good* you'll get twice as many results in your life as when you focus on the word *bad.* The really good news is that high-energy words seem to exhibit a field of dominance over low-energy words, which is why we eventually revert to optimism.

So, how can we describe something less than good without using the word *bad*? You may have noticed that I said *not good* instead of *bad* earlier. If you think of *not good*, it doesn't have the same squirmy effect in your stomach as the word *bad*, does it? That's because your unconscious mind cannot compute something that is "not." For example, do not think of a white elephant; do not imagine the number 167. In order for you to "not" think or imagine something, you have to think or imagine it first!

Your unconscious, or inner mind thinks in images or symbols, so structure your language to create images in your mind about what you *want* to happen, or what you desire. How do you bring your inner and outer world into alignment? *The first step is to change your internal and external speech patterns.* Transform your thinking and language patterns to bring you the magic of creative and transformative power.

Switch!

"Switch" is the word I use to remind myself to notice that I am using low-energy words rather than high-energy ones. It's great fun to have a "switch buddy" so that you can remind each other to use high-energy words. In my trainings and workshops I often ask the participants to play a switch game where they actually get points for catching someone else; they also give up a point each time they use a low-energy word. They can regain points if they catch themselves before their partner or group does. Simply by becoming more consciously aware of the words being used, attitudes change and relationships improve dramatically. Once you are in the practice of switching low-energy words to high-energy words, it will become second nature. To get you going, here are some common phrases that have been switched:

- "That's not bad" becomes "That's *quite good.*"
- "No problem" becomes "*You're very welcome.*"
- "That's bad" becomes "*That's not good.*"
- "Don't worry" becomes "*You'll be fine.*"
- "Put some effort into it" becomes "*Let's put some energy into it.*"
- "It's too hard" becomes "*It's not easy.*"

- "I'm sick" becomes "*I don't feel well.*"
- "I forgot" becomes "*I didn't remember.*"
- "I've been working hard" becomes "I've been *working well.*"
- "Don't cry" becomes "*That's right.*"

This last switch is an interesting one because it gives the child (or adult) permission to express and release the emotion, which is important; you'll find out why in chapter five.

If you find it less than easy to replace a low-energy word such as *difficult*, or *hard*, replace the word with *interesting*: "I'm finding this ... *interesting.*" You'll have many interesting sentences coming out of your mouth soon! Another switch sentence is: "I've got a great opportunity for growth," or, "I'm learning some lessons right now." *Puzzle* is also a good switch word. "I'm looking for a solution" works very well too.

Here are some more tips for successful switching. Remember that you aren't just switching your words; you're switching on your life!

1. Speak in *the now* as though it has already happened (and be realistic so that the conscious mind believes that it's possible): "It's easy for me to have a wonderful relationship now," (Rather than: "I *will have* a wonderful relationship." The unconscious mind is happy to believe that a wonderful relationship will happen sometime in the future, so there is no immediate need for it to respond).

2. Whenever you are planning something that you want to succeed, add a *health* connection: "My new venture is successful now because with more money in the bank I can relax more and be healthier." The unconscious mind's prime directive is to preserve the health and well-being of the body. (You'll read more about the conscious and unconscious mind in chapter three.)

3. Use the words "because" and "now" as often as you can. The conscious mind likes the word because *because* it answers the question "Why?" The unconscious likes *now* because it's like pressing the word "enter" on your keyboard. It jumps straight into action.

4. Clear *don't* [do something] from your dealings with other people. For example, "Don't drop that on the floor" switches to "Hold that carefully."

5. Clear *have to, could have*, and *should* from your self-talk, such as "I should do my work now." Those words imply obligation; resentment on some level is the underlying emotion. Switch to "I'm ready to do my work now."

6. Clear the word "try" from your vocabulary—we use the word in hypnotherapy to ensure that someone fails! "I'm trying to be successful" switches to "I'm more successful every day."

7. Clear *but* from your vocabulary. *But* can imply judgment. Replace it with *and*. For example, "You did that well, but you need to correct the spelling" becomes "You did that well and perhaps you can just check your spelling?" *But* is also a word that's usually followed by an excuse for not making changes: "I'd like to exercise, but . . ."

8. State what something *isn't* on purpose. For example, "This is really *hard*" becomes (think *switch*!) "This is really *not easy*." By thinking *switch* you automatically go to a high-energy key word.

9. Make a point of consciously using high-energy words such as *gratitude, laughter, kindness, love, abundance, success, joy, freedom, power*, and *health* in your everyday speaking and thoughts. Choose one word and then write it, use it, act on it, and live and breathe it for the whole day.

Switch! Body and Nourishment Words

Can you think yourself slim? Absolutely! Ask someone to listen to you as you talk about your body or eating habits, to make you conscious of the words you use. Then write down replacement phrases to change how you speak and think. Carry the piece of paper with you; refer to it and add to it.

- "Diet" becomes *"eating plan"* or *"nourishment plan."*
- "Fat" becomes *"not slim."*

- "Junk food" becomes "*empty filler food.*"
- "I'm feeling guilty about eating too much" becomes "*How interesting that I chose chocolate. How else can I nourish myself today?*"
- "I shouldn't eat all of this" becomes "*I'll eat just half of this.*"
- "I shouldn't be eating this cake" becomes "*It's fine to have a small piece of this.*"
- "I was bad today" becomes "*I didn't do very well today. I'm doing better from now on.*"
- "I'm feeling down" becomes "*I'm clearing some emotions right now.*"

Power your thoughts to direct your destiny. Switch on your life. Have fun finding replacement words or phrases for all negative key words. It takes a short time to make it work so that you go straight into the high-energy space without going first into the low-energy. It's very much like learning a new language. Initially you translate from one word or phrase to another, and then it becomes automatic. How do you know when the switch is on? You know when you feel happy (instead of defensive) as others point out your low-energy words! At that point, you are truly approaching the paradigm shift that will clear your language and bring fabulous changes to your life.

Change Happens

Change is the one constant in life; you are not even the same person you were two minutes ago. So when you initiate and direct energy well, which happens when you use high-energy words, you create a dynamic force that quantum-leaps you to success. The rate of propulsion for clear decision-making directly depends on five things:

1. Clear Intent

Why are you doing it? What are you intending to create? The more specific that you are in your intent, the better the results.

2. **Creativity and a Positive Plan of Action**

How do you intend to do it? How practical is it? How flexible are you?

3. **Timing**

When exactly are you going to start, and how long will it take?

4. **Heightened Emotion**

This is the magical ingredient for speeding up the process. It actually accompanies the changes taking place, as triggers set off different emotions in various proportions along the journey. This magic element makes the process more like a matrix than a sequence.

5. **Gratitude and Flexibility**

Whatever the results, celebrate when you reach 80 percent of your goals. If you want to buy and live in a three-bedroom house and you save enough for a two-bedroom house instead, celebrate how far you've come. If you don't manage any changes at all, go back to number one and rethink your strategy.

What strategy do you have for making successful choices to lead you to the right decisions? Do you use the same strategy for every decision, or are your decisions made on gut feel, or instinct? It's been proven that the most successful people in life make decisions instinctively and act on them quickly. Researchers at the University of Hertfordshire in the United Kingdom concluded that high achievers almost always act on their instincts better then anyone else. Instincts are increased when the conscious and unconscious minds work as a synchronized team.

Become a Thought Billionaire— Switch On Your Billionaire Mind

The emotional impact of words profoundly influences the way you communicate and attract success. For every low-energy word you say or think, the best that you can hope for is that the high-energy words you say or think simply replace or equalize the low ones. You can get away with saying or thinking two low-energy key words for every one high-energy word and end up with a zero balance. On the other hand, if you actually switch the low-energy words with high-energy words, something amazing happens.

Here's a little challenge—find the low-energy key words and limiting beliefs in this conversation:

"Good morning, John! How are you?"

"Not bad. I was pretty sick over Christmas and I'm still trying to shake it off. I always get sick at this time of year. It gets me really depressed."

"Poor you! That sucks. Did you get that flu that's going around? It's a really nasty one this time. Everyone's catching it—it seems to last for weeks because you think it's gone and then it comes back. It's hard to get rid of. Anyway, I've got the book you ordered. It's a bit expensive—twenty-five dollars, I'm afraid."

"Oh! I'm a bit broke right now so do you mind if I get the money to you after I get paid next week, or will a postdated check do?"

"Don't worry. I know it's really hard right now. The economy's always down every January. Whatever works for you is fine."

"Thanks very much, Linda."

"No problem. See you later."

"Bye!"

There are at least eighteen low-energy key words in this conversation (depending on the *tone* of voice used, there could be many more) and two limiting decisions (for example, "The economy's always down every January"—not necessarily true, but a nice excuse for not managing money well). There are six high-energy words: *good, pretty, money, works, fine,* and *thanks.* So, that's six high-energy words to eighteen low; proportionately a ratio of 1:3. Yet, when I keyed in those same words on the Internet, there were many, many more Web sites for high-energy words than for low-energy ones.

This suggests that the overall influence of each high-energy word is much higher than that of a low-energy word. In fact, the word "good" is the one with the most impact. "Hard" is the word that carries the most weight on the low-energy side. That's a great reason to clear the word "hard" from your language patterns (use "not good" instead, to send your unconscious mind on a search for good things). Other words to clear from your language patterns include: *worry, nasty, problem.*

Let's redo that encounter using all high-energy key words and leaving out limiting decisions:

> "*Good* morning, John. Are you *well*?"
>
> "Actually, I'm much *better*. I was not *well* at Christmas so I've decided to get *healthy* for the New Year."
>
> "*Great*! I wish you *success*. I've got *terrific* news for you— the book you ordered has arrived. It's twenty-five dollars."
>
> "*Wonderful*! Can I collect it next week? I'll have *more money* by then!"
>
> "Sure! Whatever *works* for you is *fine*. I'll see you soon."
>
> "*Thanks a million*, Linda."
>
> "You're very *welcome*, John."
>
> "Bye!"

In this high-energy conversation, the words that carry the most impact, in order from most to least, are: *new, well* (mentioned twice), *good, great, better, sure, thanks, welcome, works, fine, million, success, wonderful, healthy,* and *terrific*. The total number of key words in the first conversation is twenty-four (both high and low-energy), versus sixteen key words in this second conversation. However, note that *all* of the second conversation's key words are high-energy words.

You gain access exponentially to billions more high-energy results simply by switching from low to high. That's an amazing amount of hidden wealth in your words. You're a thought *billionaire!*

Notice, too, how much more economical language becomes when the low-energy words are not there. Productive key words propel your thoughts—and therefore your results—forward and upward as they resonate to a much higher frequency, energizing your life. Your success is in the bank, so to speak, as your mind has direct access to the generative effect of high-energy thinking.

Just Breathe

Deep breathing is one of the best ways to harmonize your mind and increase your inner power. Here is an exercise to awaken and expand your energy that I call "Seven, Seven, Eleven."

1. Breathe in for a count of seven.
2. Hold for a count of seven.
3. Breathe out for a count of eleven.
4. Breathe with your whole body. Breathe in with the rhythm of the room.
5. Breathe out, releasing nonsupportive emotions or ideas. Breathe with the rhythm of the land and the sea. Breathe with the rhythm of the earth and the stars. Breathe with the rhythm of the universe itself.
6. Form a circle of light with the breath, which flows through and around your whole being.
7. Release the past with the outward breath, preserving all of the positive messages and lessons.
8. Reclaim your awesome magnificence as you breathe in again.

You can do this exercise any time to increase your energy and self-confidence. It's particularly good in the morning as you awake or in the evening before you sleep, because you are most in touch with your unconscious mind at that point and your breathing strengthens the connection. You can even make a habit of deep breathing as you're waiting at a traffic light.

To develop your intuitive decision-making instincts further, record the following script and listen to it as you do the deep breathing:

With every breath, with every beat of your heart you may ... just let go now. Breathe deeply—and that deep breathing increases the rate of your metabolism, enriching the body with oxygen—as you begin to feel lighter and lighter now, awakening the senses as you begin to search for the answer inside ... the body. Will you feel the shift deep inside now ... or upon awakening?

Searching, surrendering to that great wisdom inside yourself as you find yourself remembering. What is the question that will allow you to move into joy now or in the next few moments? Direct your unconscious mind to send you the answer to make you happy and free.

Back over the years, over the months, smaller and smaller: nine, eight, seven, six, five, four, three months and fully formed, seven weeks and you have a heartbeat. As you remember now, becoming smaller and lighter, smaller and lighter, remembering back to when you used to breathe liquid and were fed through a cord attached to your abdomen. Feeling connected ... to an ocean of inner knowledge. The ocean is made up of the same ninety-six elements that make up your body now. Remember back to living and breathing that water.

And find yourself now ... as you go deeper and deeper inside to the source: to the quantum space between the cells, which is pure light ... becoming lighter and lighter, floating back to the dawn of existence. Programmed from within, moving forward in a self-contained, ongoing process of growth and development. You know the answer—you always did.

As you awaken, you feel different, as though you're more connected to the source of your intelligence and understanding of life. Success is searching for you, as you are searching for success. Ask your unconscious mind to search for people who can help you on your quest for happiness and bring them into your life as though by magic. Optimism comes easily to you. Open your eyes, happy and smiling for no good reason, to a brand new you.

By directing your mind back to before you were born, you reconnect with the blueprint of perfection that began this life, reminding yourself of your innately optimistic nature and your inherent ability to resolve questions.

Are You Fixed or Flowing?

Now that you have some new life tools and are more aware, it's time to delve deeper into the transformation of your life. Responsibility for change begins with ... you guessed it ... you! Life brings you better presents when you *initiate* change. Do you choose to be *re*active or *pro*active?

Imagine that you are in an empty room, in the dark. You have been told that there is a flashlight somewhere in the room and that your job is to turn on the light to find the door so that you can get out. Do you:

1. Run around and shout for help?
2. Get on your hands and knees and systematically search for the flashlight?
3. Search the walls to find a light switch?
4. Not bother looking for the flashlight because you know that if you feel the walls there's a door handle somewhere?
5. Think about it before doing anything hasty?

The choice you make will be determined by how successful you were in making previous decisions and will show what memories you have stored in the files of your inner mind. How outside the box, or how cautious were you in your thought processes? Clearly the length of time you take to get out of the room will be determined by how flexible you are, just as how flexible you are will determine how successful you are in life. I truly believe that free will always win over "fate."

For some people, initiating change is not easy. Sandi had been a friend of mine for fifteen years. She was always smiling, cheerful, and happy to give advice—whether you needed it or not. She had no children of her own, so she treated everyone as though she were their mother. She always insisted that she was fine, so no one knew that she was actually very lonely.

Six weeks before Christmas in 2000, three months before her fiftieth birthday, she left work one day feeling unwell, went home, and was rushed to the hospital for emergency surgery for colon cancer. Her bowel had burst. By Christmas she was still in intensive care, unable to speak because of a breathing tube down her throat. In spite of Sandi's physical state the nurses loved her, and one of the female doctors was keen to go ahead with chemotherapy because she was so resilient. Sandi, even without her voice, was larger than life.

Instead of giving her gifts that Christmas, we asked everyone who knew her to tell us what made her special. We wrote the words on three huge pieces of poster board. We took them into Sandi's room and read them aloud, after singing holiday carols. Some comments were funny, some poignant, some loving, and some cheery. Everyone had good things to say about her sense of humor, her helpfulness, and her capability. Tears streamed down Sandi's face as she listened. We left when she was ready to sleep, and I'll always remember the sweet smile in her eyes. She knew that she was loved that day. Words do have the power to bring light into people's lives.

I never saw Sandi conscious again. The next day a new doctor arrived in her room with some students. Her sister later told us that Sandi had asked, by writing on a piece of paper, when she would be leaving the hospital. The doctor simply said dismissively that she would never leave and would be dead before the New Year. His words were so unkind, although probably true, that Sandi slid into a coma that night. She died four days later on New Year's Eve, late in the evening. We were all keenly aware of the power of words that Christmas. Fortunately, before her passing, Sandi had been given an opportunity very rarely presented to someone: to know that she had made a difference. Since then I've handled life, and the changes and decisions life brings, like a precious gift.

Recap

1. You already have all the resources you need to be a Master Communicator.
2. Always talk and think about what you want your *results* to be: clearly and with intention, using high-energy words. Your words are gifts that you give to others, and you receive limitless bounty from them for yourself.

3. Practice decision-making using One-to-Ten to learn how to trust your own judgment and make clear decisions.

4. Start making changes in your life now, beginning with "fun."

5. Think of every word you speak as though it's a key word you're typing into a search engine on the Internet. What results would you get back? What results are you getting from the words you are thinking and speaking?

6. Think switch! If you catch yourself saying or thinking a low-energy word, immediately replace it. For example, "I feel *horrible* today" (switch to a high-energy phrase): "I don't *feel great.*"

7. Breathe and meditate to clear your channels to higher consciousness.

Chapter One Action Plan

1. Simply choose one low-energy word and clear it from your vocabulary now. Practice switching from low-energy phrases to high-energy phrases, using the list in the appendix.

2. Do the deep breathing exercise right now: *Seven, Seven, Eleven.*

3. Find a "switch buddy." Switch each other's language for seven days and notice the difference in how you feel about yourself and others.

4. Talk to someone in the next hour, in person or on the phone, and tell them what you really like (or love) about them, or how proud you are of them.

5. Google *www.google.com/trends* and type in "sad, happy." You'll see a graph showing how often the words appeared in the news. You'll also find out which countries most often searched those words over the past two years. You can type in individual words or two contrasting words. The graphs and country lists are very interesting. (Who knew that Australians hold three of the top ten spots for the most frequent searches for the word "depression"?)

6. Plan something fun to do today or tonight for half an hour or more. Then do it.

2

The Power of Self-Worth

*Search deep inside now to discover the wealth of treasure
and talents that already belong to you. Then listen;
it's the joyful sound of your heart singing.*

Free to Be Me

Your self-worth is 100 percent reliant on your inner dialogue (your thoughts and your words). There are only two kinds of thoughts: thoughts that empower you and those that don't! So how do you speak to yourself, about yourself, inside your mind? Is your self-talk supportive and encouraging? Or are you busy repeating to yourself the numerous negative words or phrases that we all heard before we were even seven years old? ("Don't touch that/Didn't I tell you/When are you going to learn ...?")

Have you ever noticed how much we are drawn to people who have that elusive quality we call charisma? What is it about someone who displays confidence and success that makes them so attractive? It's the sense that they know themselves well; one feels that they would be able to tackle any project with assurance. They really appear to enjoy who they are, and they also make others feel important and interesting. You know intuitively that they are true to themselves and feel worthy.

True self-worth is about feeling completely free to be your amazing self; trusting your strength of character and your own judgment. Why is self-worth so important? Because when you approve of yourself, you stay calm and move easily forward toward success, with spirit and courage, making clear decisions, confident of the results. You become more resilient, self-reliant, and self-sufficient. Self-worth is how you measure inner strength. As a therapist, I soon realized that just about every person who came to see me was incongruent about self-esteem on some level. It's the root of why people don't succeed as well as they could—and why, when congruent, they do!

Shani, an international fashion model for ten years, was very happy that I introduced her to the power of words. Tall, slim, and beautiful, she has "the look" of a model. She told me at one of my seminars that she now realized that she was actually perpetu-ating negativity with her self-talk. Her work had slowed down in the last few years, and she told me that she had assumed it was because she was getting older and gaining a little weight.

After the seminar, she applied herself to switching her words so that they became empowering to herself and to others. She stopped putting others down and consciously changed her thinking. She called me three months later and told me with excitement,

> It's amazing! I started to receive a lot more compliments (at work and otherwise) on my beauty, despite not having changed my skin care or hairstyle or updating my wardrobe. I found myself feeling and looking more attractive. This may seem far-fetched, yet it is so true! I actually got back into working in modeling again. I've found myself busier with friends, and a lot more people want to be around me. I feel like "the life of the party," and a lot more dynamic and in control of my environment. I just feel different; others tell me that I seem happier, like I really want to be here. I can hear the old word patterns and am more aware of how the

words are not liberating. When I listen to others I actually hear them more clearly. I feel like I am taken more seriously and "liked" better, even when I speak my mind. I feel empowered and, yes, I really feel more beautiful! I smile more and others around me are responding to my energy.

The best thing about changing your inner and outer talk is that others know that you're different and nicer, but they can't put a finger on why you suddenly seem like a ray of sunshine!

You Are So Amazing

Every day is a new adventure. Every day is an opportunity to live life to the fullest—a fresh opportunity to create the new you and to celebrate who you are. You are unique. You are the only person in the world who has your experience and the understanding of life the way you live it. You deserve to be here. You are already a winner. It's time to live the life you always dreamed about. You are important. We need your wonderful spark to complete the circle of energy that unites us all.

Compassion is uniquely human; it's the ability to understand and sympathize with another's perspective by putting yourself in someone else's shoes. You give a gift to someone when you empathize. We all love to give; however, allowing yourself to receive is essential if you want to succeed, because enormous rewards come when you open up the channel of energy we call abundance.

Jim came to me for a private therapy session to improve his self-confidence. He had invented a computer software system and was intent on getting it marketed. He had contacts but was reluctant to ask for help. When I asked him why, he replied that he was a giver, not a taker. I asked him how it felt when he gave. He came back with, "Wonderful! That's what makes life worth living—the feeling that you've made a difference in someone's life."

I pointed out that by not asking others for help, he was actually not allowing someone else to experience that great feeling. He looked startled. "Wow! I really have to rethink that one. So I need to think of it as a gift to them when I ask for help?" Exactly. Every time you give to others, you benefit yourself. Every time you accept help, you empower humanity by connecting with and increasing the universal communication network.

Jim also had very little physical energy, as he was spending most of his time assisting others instead of directing his own life. When self-worth is not as good as it should be, people tend to be perfectionists, with unrealistic expectations of how they want others to behave. They tend to project outward, to gain approval by being over-nurturing to others, thus leaving themselves with fewer resources.

I taught Jim how to do the One-to-Ten decision-making strategy the next time he felt the need to help someone, so that he would know if he had enough energy and motivation. He also decided to make two phone calls to people he had helped in the past who would know of ways to market his product.

Your relationship with someone else can only work if you have a good relationship with yourself. You know how much courage it took to come this far. Know that you are good, imaginative, conscientious, and pure of heart. You are strong, funny, friendly, and trustworthy. If you don't know this yet, then there's simply something more you need to find out about yourself!

Believing that you *deserve* to receive is a large part of self-worth and abundance. When you feel deserving, you give yourself permission to receive all of the treats that life has to offer, with joy. Get ready to receive abundance on every level as you move toward balance from a good foundation of freedom of choice.

How do you know if you truly love and accept yourself? One way is to simply heighten your observation of people and events that you attract into your life. Self-worth keeps you on track, tuned in, and connected, so if something in your life is not flowing, that means that there's something that is not congruent with your map of the world. As you send out words and thoughts, your unconscious mind, in effect, rushes out to retrieve what you focus on! It's eager to let you know what needs to be examined, or resolved, in order to bring your energy into balance.

Life is purely a mirror, a reflection of what you feel and believe about yourself right now. Even if you aren't sure that you believe this yet, by pretending that it's the truth, you begin the journey of self-exploration and reflection; this leads you to knowing yourself completely and is the prelude to self-worth. When you meet someone who's doing wonderfully well, remember to congratulate yourself for being on the right path. This propels you further on your journey to align you with your own inner true north. Then abundance will flow into your life like a waterfall.

The second way to think about the question is how *well* you truly love and accept yourself. Ask yourself this: "On a scale of one to ten (one being low, ten being high), how much of my heart feels truly connected?" You can contextualize this question by adding, "... in the context of career," or "... in the context of relationships."

This may seem like an odd question, but the truth is that the extent to which you feel connected with others is a mirror of your connection with yourself—your self-worth. People with a low self-concept often feel that they have a space somewhere in their heart where they dwell alone. If that's the case, ask yourself a question that will be easier for you to answer: "On a scale of one to ten, how much of my heart feels that I dwell alone?"

Whatever you get for an answer, view the results with curiosity and a desire to find out what more you need to discover to feel totally connected. The exercises that follow in this chapter are designed to help you begin to fill in the blanks.

If you don't always get what you want, it's often because your goals are not aligned with your values in life. Core values are intrinsic to you, and they are what give meaning to your existence. When your life and purpose are aligned with your values, you feel that you are in a state of grace. It's like finding the perfect pitch on a tuning fork and resonating with it. Being in tune with your life then allows your destiny to flow along smoothly. That's when the magic happens. There are words such as *honesty*, *fairness*, *truth*, *integrity*, and *faith* that are global core values, and values such as *prosperity*, *prestige*, or a *comfortable home* that are more contextual. You also have personal values that you learned from your parents or friends. To truly experience and enjoy your reason for being here, it's important to know what's

Key Values and States

Ability
Abundance
Acceptance
Accuracy
Achievement
Acknowledgement
Adventure
Altruism
Balance
Beauty
Brotherhood
Charity
Children
Comfort
Communication
Compassion
Competence
Contentment
Conquest
Cooperation
Courage
Creativity
Culture
Dignity
Discovery
Duty
Ease
Energy
Enjoyment
Excitement
Fame
Family
Forgiveness
Freedom
Friendship
Fun

Glory
God
Goodness
Greatness
Growth
Happiness
Health
Honesty
Honor
Hope
Humility
Independence
Individuality
Innocence
Innovation
Integrity
Intimacy
Joy
Justice
Kindness
Knowledge
Law-abidance
Leaving a mark
Leisure
Love
Making a difference
Mastery
Maturity
Money
Nature
Originality
Patience
Peace of mind
Pleasure
Popularity
Positivity

Power
Prestige
Pride
Privacy
Property
Prosperity
Purpose
Reason
Respect
Responsibility
Risk
Romance
Routine
Safety
Security
Self-control
Self-esteem
Self-interest
Service
Sex
Spirituality
Strength
Success
Support
Surrender
Talent
Teamwork
Toys
Treasure
Trust
Truth
Wealth
Wisdom
Working with
  people

of value to you, because when you understand and adhere to the motivation behind what you do, you readily achieve your heart's desires.

When asked what they want, many people say, "To be happy" or "To be rich." Being rich or happy is a state of being, not a value, although happiness and riches may well come because you follow your values as you pursue your dreams.

How do you find your values? Read the list on the previous page. Highlight or pick out your ten most important states or values. Go through quickly and allow your unconscious mind to pick out the ones that jump out at you.

Of those you've picked, which is the one that is absolutely essential to your well-being? You can only choose one from the whole list. If you had that top one fulfilled, which is the next most important? And the next? Order your values so that you have your top five to seven picks.

This next task is most interesting. It's sometimes easier if you ask someone else to help you with this one. Let's say you are asking yourself about career values, and you work at a bank as a computer programmer. In this case, your original list of essentials might be:

1. Money
2. Prestige
3. Making a difference
4. Enjoyment
5. Creativity
6. Working with people

The first task is to take the top value and ask yourself, "In the context of my career, would it be all right for me to have *money* and not have *prestige*?"

The answer might be yes, so then ask, "Would it be all right for me to have *money* and not *make a difference*, in the context of career?" The answer might be no, so suddenly your values need to be realigned. Ask yourself the same question for all of the other values in turn, going down the list and reordering them as their importance is revealed. When you have found your number one value, go on to the next word down the list and start again.

So you would ask: "In the context of my career, would it be all right for me to have *prestige* and not have *enjoyment* of my work?" Probably not, so again, the order will change (although, for someone like the Queen of England, a high-ranking value of duty would override the need for enjoyment).

You might end up with this order of importance:

1. Making a difference
2. Working with people
3. Creativity
4. Enjoyment
5. Money
6. Prestige

That order would certainly make you rethink what you want to do for a living. At the bank, a job you might enjoy that would adhere to those values could be as a training manager or a mortgage broker. Success has different meanings for different people. True success is when you feel great about who you are, what you do, and what you have. Amazingly, this is the same as when you have true self-worth.

Change Your Internal Dialogue: It's Time to Make Friends—With Yourself!

Are you ready to write your own self-love script? It's the one about the authentic you. Do you truly know your best qualities? How do you find out? Read on! For the following exercise:

Please write your answers to the list below, numbered 1 to 7 on a separate piece of paper. You'll need a handheld tape recorder or karaoke machine to record your own voice: the voice your unconscious mind loves to listen to the most!

1. **Make a list of your mother's *best* qualities**, as though you are speaking to her (even if she's not here any longer). For example: emotions, talents, practicality, looks, intelli-

gence, people skills, determination, sense of humor, education, etc. State it like this is the way she *is* (without using low-energy words):

You are _____

2. **Make a list of your father's *best* qualities:**
   You are _____

3. **Who is the person or animal you love the most? List their best qualities:**
   You are _____

4. **Who or what kind of person do you most admire in the world?** (This can be someone you don't know, someone famous for instance):
   I admire you because you are _____
   _____

5. **Describe your ideal romantic partner:**
   You are _____
   You are also _____

6. **What things do you most admire about *yourself*?**
   Look in a mirror if you need some ideas for this one.
   You are _____

7. **Now list ten things or people you are *grateful* for in your life today.**
   I am grateful for _____
   _____
   because _____

You should end up with a list that reads like this (fill in the blanks):

1. (Mother) You are ...
2. (Father) You are ...
3. (Person or animal) You are ...
4. (Others) I admire you because you are ...
5. (Romantic Partner) You are ...
   You are also ...
6. (Self) You are ...
7. I am grateful for ... because ...

This is the basis of your script for the authentic you. What you notice and like in other people are *your own best qualities*.

Speak and record (pausing for two silent counts between each sentence):

 As you close your eyes, relaxing more deeply than you've ever relaxed before, imagine yourself in a beautiful, safe place in nature. Feel your face softening as you breathe and just ... let ... go. There's a gentle breeze playing with your hair.

Perhaps imagine yourself in a forest, where there's water bubbling from a nearby brook, or by a lakeside, where a stream gushes over rocks to meet the lake.

Make your way to the water, where you may be surprised to find, as you observe your reflection, that you seem to have a new glow around you. This is the real you, the authentic you. The sun is shining and there's a rainbow of light arching down from the sky, shining through the water droplets.

If you were now to imagine an angel or God as a color, what color would that be? (Pause)

Notice now how a shaft of this glowing color is infusing your entire head, shoulders, and body with a new feeling of health and vitality as you become aware of how radiant you look today. And you know as you reconnect now with that inner and outer light that you are that light. You have the knowledge and wisdom of eternity in every cell of your body.

(Now read aloud your 1 to 6 results—all the best qualities of yourself.)

1. *You are ...*
2. *You are ...*
3. *You are ...*
4. *I admire you because you are ...*
5. *You are also ...*
6. *You know you are ...*

As you remember the authentic you—the true, pure, original you—you may recognize your inner spirit of truth and bravery. You may recognize now the strength of character, honor, and trust again.

You are breathing, you are living, and you are relaxing into pure joy as you remember now a time in your life when you truly liked yourself. Just recall one moment when you knew that you were doing something admirable.
(Pause)

If you were to find a place in your physical body right now where that wonderful memory is stored, where would that be?
(Pause)

Bringing your awareness to the one cell that holds the most of that memory, observe, see, feel, or sense a whirling vortex of power spreading outward from that one cell, reminding each and every cell in your heart, chest, liver, lungs, and whole body of this delightful feeling.

Observing now every cell "high-fiving" every other cell in your . . . shoulders, neck, head, face, arms, and hands. The intensity spreading now through your organs, spine, hips, thighs, knees, calves, and feet—every cell singing and celebrating with release and freedom.

With pride and a delicious sense of satisfaction, you notice that every cell in your whole body is tingling with excitement. Life is wonderful. You realize suddenly that you are grateful. You are grateful for sunshine and laughter . . . for the trees, birds, and flowers.

You are blessed.

You are grateful for . . . (insert word list—number seven)

You can trust yourself now.

Just before you drift off into a deep, deep sleep every night, you may be reminded of something nice that you did today. Perhaps you may remember something good that someone said about you.

Perhaps, however you sleep, deeply or peacefully, dreaming or not dreaming, you awaken every morning feeling great, fully revitalized on every level, knowing that today is a new chance to start afresh, to begin something new. Today is a day to live life with laughter and fun, delighted to be alive.

It's a day to remember to love and accept yourself.

Now, when you are ready, open your eyes to a brand new you.

You may decide that "I am ..." works better for you than "You are. . . ." This is just personal preference. Simply choose the language that you enjoy listening to the most. You can also add in any other suggestions to make you feel great. Listen to this every day and you'll very quickly start to think of yourself in a whole new light.

Let Go, Let Flow, Learn to Say No, and Then Reward Yourself!

Self-worth also involves being able to set boundaries. When we truly value who we are, we understand that it's good for us to have needs and desires, and to take care of ourselves. When we value ourselves, we can value others more completely. You may or may not change your personality overnight, so here's a step-by-step method for learning to say no:

"Sue, could you please come and help me move on Saturday?"
Sue thinks, "Oh no! Not in my wildest dreams!"
Sue says, "Of course, it will be a pleasure. I'll arrange the babysitting and bring some hot dogs, and we'll have a barbecue later!"
Sue *thinks*, "I can't believe I said that!"
Sue will do the job, ending up feeling displeased and then disappointed if her friend doesn't even offer to pay for the hot dogs.

What's the way out? Remember the One-to-Ten exercise for decision-making: "How good is it for me to ...?" (1 to 10) Remember: five or below and the answer is no!

Option 1 (One-to-Ten Decision)

Sue thinks: "How good is it for me to help Ann move to her new house?"

Sue's response: 5 or 6 out of 10 (not a good enough response to spend the whole day doing it!).

Sue replies to Ann: "Okay, I can give you three hours. Is 1 to 4 PM all right? I need to get back home after that."

Sue has now shortened the time so that Ann can probably get someone else to do part of the work. Ann is too busy to thank Sue with flowers or a card; she's moving, and we all know how interesting that can be without having to wonder whether a helpful friend feels validated! Sue needs to reward *herself*. Kids do this instinctively.

So, as Sue responds, her reward should already be formulating in her head: a walk, a massage, a hot bath, a special treat. This directly lets the friend off the hook so that no resentment can form. If Ann later remembers and comes up with the flowers or a thank you note, it's received as a *bonus*, not an essential part of the equation.

Reward List

1. Walk or jog in the fresh air
2. Listen to music
3. Go and work out
4. Have a massage
5. Golf
6. Eat something sensual: "I eat this with *love!*"
7. Buy new clothes
8. Book a trip
9. Put your feet up for ten minutes
10. Watch a special television program
   ... And so on.

Nurturing yourself is part of enjoying your individuality. It's also important to allow yourself solitude every day to replenish your soul and make the connection with the inner mind. Take time for yourself as you create your life, because taking your time is essential for a healthy body and spirit, in order to keep the "well" full. When you feel great you have so much more to give to yourself and other people.

Option 2

Sue thinks, "How good is it for me to help Ann move?" The response is 2 out of 10. If she still finds herself saying yes, the reward needs to be *very* big in order to console herself for doing something that she *really* doesn't want to do (a new set of clothes, a day off, three hours of doing nothing, a cinema/theater outing). The best response? "Oh Ann, Saturday doesn't work for me." ("I can't" only leads to "Why not?" and Sue will find herself not telling the truth!) This is the halfway stage to learning to say no.

After just a short time of practice, you will find that saying no just becomes easier. By defining your boundaries, the time you would normally spend doing things with a heart that's less than open is returned to you, like a gift to yourself. This time can be used to replenish and boost your internal state. What do you do with all this extra time? Have fun and enjoy yourself! You can begin, if you like, by sustaining your positive state with some optimism and mood boosters. Below is a list of ideas for helping you to replenish.

Twelve Quick Tips to Re-la-a-ax...

1. Breathe. Take four deep breaths. Close your eyes and do the Seven–Seven–Eleven breath from the previous chapter.
2. Play with your dog or another pet; this has been proven to increase serotonin levels, which are calming.
3. Begin the day with fiber, such as bran or oatmeal. It helps to regulate *cortisol* (the steroid stress hormone). Orange juice (or any vitamin C drink) has the same effect. During the day, snack on foods with high levels of magnesium, such as peanuts, almonds, sunflower seeds, and pumpkin seeds, to boost your mood by increasing serotonin.
4. Close your eyes and remember the happiest moment of your life. Imagine where that moment might be stored in your body (simply choose a place now). Then find the one cell in the middle of that area that's holding the greatest intensity of the happy moment. Imagine that one cell as a little smiley person high-fiving every other cell throughout your body.
5. Doodle while you work—this sends your brain into *alpha*, which is similar to a state of meditation. It takes you into more peaceful, higher brain functions.

6. Sing! The sound waves trigger alpha relaxation and the breathing changes encourage your brain to take time off. Taking singing lessons also improves your breathing and self-confidence.

7. Dance to music. In fact, any kind of fun movement will stimulate serotonin levels.

8. Meditate or do self-hypnosis for fifteen or twenty minutes every day. Twenty minutes of hypnosis has been proven to equal four hours of sleep.

9. Laugh. Be happy. Watch a funny movie.

10. Keep your chin up. Literally. This puts you physiologically into the higher brain, the happy brain. So does the color blue. Look at a blue sky or hang a beautiful picture with some blue in it, above eye level, wherever you normally spend most of your day.

11. Stand up straight, look up at the ceiling, take a deep breath, and hold it as you tense every muscle and think or say "Yes! Yes! Yes!" Then release and let go.

12. Write "ME!" in your daily schedule to remind you to take time for yourself.

The following two Magic of the Mind exercises change either your internal state or your outward physiology so that you can access good feelings at will. This first one is a great way to get happy instantly.

Magic of the Mind One

Close your eyes and remember a time when you felt really excited about an event in your life. See what you see, feel what you feel, hear and taste and smell. Feel the picture come alive. Breathe it; be it. Now imagine standing outside the picture, and shrink the picture down to the size of a small, dark postage stamp. Send the stamp out to the top left-hand corner of the room. How do you feel now? Now say "WHOOSH!" aloud as you bring the picture back to you; imagine yourself stepping into it, as though you are stepping into a sunny day. Feel the powerful time again: turn up the colors, the sounds, and the feelings. Breathe it until you feel tingly and alive, then step out and repeat, shrinking the picture and sending it back up to the corner of the room. Imagine zipping back into it a few times until you feel great.

Magic of the Mind Two

Another way to access feel-good feelings is to close your hand into a fist and think "Yes!" any time you are experiencing fabulous fun or just feeling great. When you do this regularly, if you are feeling less than good at some later time, simply by closing your fist you will go immediately to a place of feeling fine.

These short exercises get easier the more you do them. The mechanical aspect of how your mind works when you direct it with words and imagination is fairly straightforward. You've found out now that you can change your state almost instantly with the words and thoughts you think to yourself.

So far we've been exploring beneath the surface somewhat, and increasing your observation skills in order to open up new possibilities. How exactly do you get to the vast resources of magic that will enable you to find the gold at the end of the rainbow? You open your mind to the potential of the quantum universe.

Quantum Mechanics

Although we each appear to be having a linear, localized experience, we are non local—we are part of the matrix of the energy field that forms the cosmos. We are so much more than we realize. For example, your hand, while it is part of you, does not describe your complete self. If you were to look more closely at each cell of your hand through a microscope, you would see that the DNA in every cell is identical to every other cell in the whole of your body. Looking even more closely, at the quantum space between each cell (the subatomic space), you would realize that you are looking at the stuff the universe is made of, making you both a microcosm and a macrocosm at the same time.

There is no reality in the absence of observation.
—The Copenhagen Interpretation of Quantum Mechanics

Classical Newtonian physics gives us a way to understand how the natural world works. It assumes that there is an order to things which, when understood, will allow us to have tools to make predictions about the natural physical world. However, during the first part of the twentieth century, scientists found a whole range of extraordinary phenomena in their laboratory experiments that didn't seem to conform to the rules of classical (action/reaction) physics.

There was something extra that the calculations of classical physics didn't explain. Scientists then began to formulate some acceptable theories for the unusual results, which now form the basis for quantum mechanics.

Quantum (from Latin *quantus*, or "how much") mechanics is the branch of physics that governs how the smallest particles behave. In this world, substance is nothing more than vibration, and all that exists is particles and waves. Quantum mechanics involves a significant reworking of the physical laws of behavior on atomic and subatomic scales, because at this level wonderfully strange things happen: for instance, an electron can be in two places at the same time.

The contributions of numerous scientists during the early part of this century culminated in 1936, in Copenhagen, with a series of papers and lectures by Neils Bohr and Werner Heisenberg, which are now more or less accepted as the "orthodox" interpretation of quantum mechanics.

One of the primary principles of quantum mechanics is that a property does not exist unless it can be measured, and that it's not easy to measure because indeterminacy is a fundamental property of the universe. Heisenberg's Uncertainty Principle states that the more variables there are, the more unpredictable the result.

In other words, nothing is real until it's measured, and there are things that we just can't measure. We know these things exist because they have an observable effect on things we *can* measure!

There is also what's known as a *hidden variable*, which does not allow us to measure results with any degree of certainty. This hidden variable acts as interference and causes an entangled state. Consequently, at the level of the quantum field, which is the name given by scientists to the distribution of energy that is constantly creating and recreating particles, just about anything becomes possible. This is an important concept to understand because this hidden variable is also the key to accessing our previously untapped personal power.

As you learn to fine-tune switching to high-energy words, you'll find yourself in the magical world of quantum potentials and hidden variables, amazed by how quickly you can change the results in your life.

As if this quantum world of possibilities weren't amazing enough, consider for a moment the stupendous capacity that our brains hold: for processing alone, the brain has one hundred trillion possible connections, each capable of calculating simultaneously. It also holds the equivalent amount of twelve hundred *terabytes* of computer memory; that's six million years worth of the *Wall Street Journal*!

Now, recall that it's through our inner, unconscious mind that we connect with and shape the energy of the universe, including the quantum field. We already have within us a "supercomputer" that can adapt to both the reliable Newtonian world and the quantum field where novel information, processing, and the ability to manifest our dreams can occur.

> *When you wish upon a word . . .*
> *all your dreams will soon be heard.*

By now, I hope that you are getting the idea that by consciously switching your words and directing your thoughts, you transform not only your perception of life but also your results. There's something more to learn here. It is something so special that when you embrace it fully, you'll have the key to direct your destiny and tap into the most amazing amount of power, joy, and happiness.

The key lies in understanding that there is infinite abundance available for all of us. Observe nature's luxury. There is more than enough air to breathe, more than enough water, more than enough food to eat. This abundance is part of your heritage. There are equally enormous amounts of love, joy, health, prosperity, and time just waiting to be claimed. Once you learn to trust the inner you completely, and are able to send out the correct message to your unconscious mind based on clear decisions and high-energy words and thoughts, you'll be able to access the riches you always dreamed of having: great health, wonderful friends, intimate relationships, wealth, happiness, and peace of mind.

Remember that success is searching for you, as you are searching for success. Love is searching for you, as you are searching for love. Wonderful people are searching for you, as you are searching for them. Prosperity and health are searching for you, as you are searching for them.

Recap

1. There are two kinds of thoughts: supportive and non-supportive.
2. Your self-concept is decided daily by how you speak to yourself.
3. You can love someone else only to the extent that you love yourself. You can connect with others when you are connected to yourself.
4. Everything you are, do, or get depends on your own self-worth.
5. Receiving is as important as giving.
6. Life is a mirror; look into it every day to find out how you're doing.
7. The three answers to requests for help:

- Yes, I'd love to.
- I'll help you for a short time.
- No, it doesn't work for me.

8. Your values align you to your inner true north.
9. Reward and fun every day are essential to your happiness.
10. Self-nurturing is essential to your growth and development. Be kind to yourself today.

Chapter Two Action Plan

1. Read the list of top, optimistic high-energy words in the appendix and choose one new word to use every day.
2. Write down your daily "to do" list and check off three essentials to do today. Which are the three most important ones? When you've done those, count any other tasks that you accomplish as a bonus. You regain a sense of self-worth and pride in your accomplishments.
3. Pick one of the things to do from the optimism/mood booster list and do it now.
4. Change your physiology by standing up, shoulders back, breathing from the top of the lungs, eyes up, and take a few deep breaths of release. This puts you instantly into high brain/happy brain/alpha state.
5. Make a list of things that you love to do, and post the list somewhere obvious in your home or office. Do one or more of these every day.
6. Consciously surround yourself with supportive people you really like and enjoy being around.

3

The Power
of Awareness

*I'm trying to free your mind, Neo. But I can only show
you the door. You're the one who must walk through it.*
—Morpheus from *The Matrix*

Word Power: The Key to Your Success

Just think about this—what would happen if every thought
you had came true? What if every fear you had came true
instantaneously? Would you choose to speak and think differently? What if everything you thought or said about others
came true for you instead? Would you think more kindly
thoughts about others? Would you treat them better than you
would otherwise?

Why is it so important for us to understand ourselves and be
aware of our thought processes? *Because we create our world with our
thoughts and words.* Every great cathedral, every new invention,
every decision ever made began with just one thought. What you
think about and focus on is what you materialize and manifest in
your life (and you always get more, the more you focus), so your

thoughts and language need to be clearly directed to produce great results. You are the Master Creator of your own life. The tools and insights in this book will help you to access and design your own blueprint for success.

Is there something you'd like to have work better in your life right now? Perhaps your career, relationships, prosperity, health, or self-esteem? To improve your situation requires one of two things: either there's simply something more that you need to know about yourself or the circumstances, or it's time to change the thoughts and words you use internally to describe the experience. So if I were to give you a gift today, it would be the gift of curiosity, to learn and grow swiftly like a young child.

You already have the internal freedom, like that of a child, to choose what comes out of your mind and your lips. Your thoughts are as real as the furniture that you're sitting on. So be careful. Your mind is listening and responding as it follows what it believes to be your desires. The words, symbols, and pictures that you choose to have in your head right now are planning your future at this very moment. There are literally thousands upon thousands of dynamic, life-affirming thoughts and words available for you to choose to think and speak.

Your happiness and the results in your life depend directly on the efficiency of the flow of communication between your outer, or conscious mind (simply what you can see, hear, feel, think, and touch), and your inner, or unconscious mind, which comprises ninety percent of who you are and controls just about everything else, including breathing, digestion, emotions, and survival mechanisms. Your inner mind is also responsible for bringing you more of whatever you focus on.

How much personal power you can generate depends on that flow of communication. If you focus on negative thoughts or use negative language (low-energy words), you dramatically slow down the speed between what you want and what you actually get. Great inner dialogue is like the switch that turns up the power, enabling you to better trust and embrace life. It allows you to accelerate your personal growth with an attitude of curiosity and experimentation, much as a child does.

As you go through life, every experience you have has an effect on the connection between your inner (unconscious) and outer (conscious) mind. Experience shapes your beliefs and your beliefs shape your identity; each influences the language you use to describe your experience. A less than happy experience might produce low-energy emotions and nonsupportive beliefs that, unless cleared, will act as an interference pattern between you and your goals. If low-energy emotions linger, your unconscious mind is attempting to let you know that something inside you is not resolved. You might think of low emotions as little clouds above your head that hide the sunshine. Clearing them is important, because just like negative language and beliefs, they slow down the response time and defer or diminish the great results that your inner (unconscious) mind is eager to bring to you.

The inner you—your inner mind—holds an "invisible blue-print of life." It represents your wonderful quantum self: all of your individual talents, abilities, present and future potentials, and possibilities. It is the "perfect" you, which we all have available to us. It is simply powerful energy. Think of a power source such as electricity. Electricity has no intrinsic quality of "good" or "bad." It does not think; it just is. However, it can be *used* for good, or not.

You can choose to use your own energy for great or uninspired results, depending on how you experience life's events. Events in your life are just that—events. You can choose to *respond* differently from now on by paying more attention to the thoughts and language you use to describe those events, and feeling very thankful that you are being given signals and signs to help you along the path toward greater happiness. The more curiosity you have to discover what thought and language patterns keep occurring, and why, the easier it is to change them.

The advice most often given to people to manifest success and direct their destiny is "Think positively." That's like telling someone who's learning a new language to simply listen carefully and hope that they can catch on! Successful thinking starts with consciously changing the very first word or thought and builds from there.

You are the teacher and instructor of your own mind. If you're not getting the response or the results in life you want, it probably means that you need to think about simplifying and clarifying your language so that your mind can better understand the message and create what you want.

Instruct Your Mind to Construct Your Life

Dr. Masaru Emoto, a Japanese researcher, has made some noteworthy discoveries about the relationship between thought and matter by using water crystals. Utilizing an extremely powerful microscope and high-speed photography in a very cold room, he photographs frozen water crystals. He discovered that the crystals change when specific and concentrated thoughts are directed at them. For example, when he presented loving words and music (written or spoken) to forming water crystals, he observed that the water developed into brilliant and colorful complex patterns, like snowflakes. Water that had low-energy thoughts directed toward it, such as negative emotions (fear, anger, and so on), had dull-colored and asymmetrical patterns. From this and similar research, it is easy to imagine how words and thoughts have a similar effect on human bodies since we are comprised of seventy percent water, as is the earth itself.

Words are how we give form and action to our thoughts, and they have enormous energy and power. You have the opportunity each time you open your mouth to turn your world and the world around you into a better place. As you begin to change your mind now by becoming actively aware of the language you use to communicate with yourself and others, you can choose to see, feel, hear, touch, think, and speak differently. Imagine, as you speak and think, how your words might affect water, and then realize that those words affect your mind and body in the same way. What messages did you send out today with your words?

I started switching low-energy words with high-energy, life-affirming word patterns years ago, and discovered firsthand with my clients that consistent speech and thought repatterning introduces immediate resonance and harmony into one's life. This in turn prepares us for tuning in to the even higher frequencies needed to produce long-term, consistent, and powerful (and quick) manifestation of our goals.

Dr. Ebi Taebi is a Canadian doctor of naturopathic medicine who specializes in cancer, chronic disease, and depression. He began consciously using high-energy words, and he reported to me that this changed his whole attitude in only three months. He observed significant changes in his patients as well. He saw "miraculous" results with depression and amazing healing results from teaching his clients to switch their words. He also gets faster outcomes in his daily practice, and his patients seem to be much more optimistic. As a happy by-product, his client base and income have also increased because people are more drawn to his sunny disposition and are delighted to recommend him to others.

View any and all events that distract you from achieving your goals as feedback telling you that you need to be more consistent in *your* thoughts and actions. The question to ask yourself is not *when* you are going to decide to clear obstacles, but *how quickly* you can meet them and surpass them. Just imagine how your life is about to improve as you choose to change your responses to events *now*, and begin to connect with and reclaim the immense power of your inner mind, opening the space for success.

Becoming aware of the words you use and making a conscious choice to change them is the first step toward creating your happy, revitalized future because it opens up your beliefs to the idea of total freedom of choice. Curiosity propels you forward; change then occurs at the unconscious level (all change is unconscious, by the way) and getting results becomes instantaneous.

> *Those who believe they can do something and those who believe they can't are both right.*
> —Henry Ford

Humans are, by nature, creators and creative. This creativity produces a high-level energy vibration in the brain, which in turn activates greater levels of vibration in the mind, eventually reaching the level of activity necessary to produce wonderful thoughts and ideas. Manifestation of all your hopes and desires begins at the highest possible vibration of energy (God, or the Universal Mind), and vibrates easily through the super conscious / collective unconscious, and into the unconscious, inner mind. Your inner, unconscious mind is directly in contact with this highest power of vibration.

Your conscious mind can only connect with the power of creation through the brain, which is the switch point between it and the unconscious, inner mind. Therefore, the more your conscious mind connects, or is in congruence with the unconscious, the more quickly your desires will manifest.

That being said, it's important to know how you can access the unconscious mind and learn how to formulate suggestions in such a way that it will listen and be encouraged to take an *active* part in your quest for a healthy, prosperous, and happy life. To do that, it's good to first understand how the conscious and the unconscious minds work.

Be Mindful of Your Conscious Mind

The conscious mind consists of approximately ten percent of your mind. It functions in a state of active *awareness*. As you are reading this page, become aware of the words on the page and its layout. You are using your logical, conscious mind to do this. The conscious mind initiates all the cognitive concepts: learned knowledge, verbal and mathematical skills, creativity, and reasoning. This particular brain function comes to fruition around the age of two, as you become more autonomous and self-aware.

There are ten important things to be aware of about your conscious mind:

1. The Conscious Mind Is Aware of What It Perceives

The conscious mind functions in a state of awareness and controls all voluntary body movements, and knows your body and its surroundings through the sense organs. All of your perceptual senses report to the conscious mind. Consciously, we perceive the world predominantly through five channels: sight, hearing, taste, touch, and smell. Visually dominant people perceive the world primarily from what they remember seeing. Auditorily dominant people remember experiences by replaying the sounds they heard. Kinesthetic people remember experiences by a smell, or by what they felt, touched, or tasted. Auditory-digital people remember what they were thinking about and what made sense to them at the time. Our experience of reality is simply the memory of what we perceived at the time; we make up stories or pictures (words and thoughts) to describe our selective version of events.

2. It Contacts Reality Through the Sense Organs

All of your sensory input is directed through electrical impulses passed along by chemical reactions through the neural pathways in your body. The brain is the switch network that directs messages from your unconscious to your conscious mind and back. By heightening your sensory acuteness, you can increase your conscious awareness and strengthen the connection between your inner and outer mind.

As you are reading, become aware of your body temperature and the room temperature, and feel the chair or surface beneath you. Make note of any colors around you and notice what you can clearly see, or what is in your peripheral vision. Notice if there are any smells around and whether they are pleasant or unpleasant. Can you hear a clock ticking? Music? Nature? Traffic? Silence? How does your mouth feel and taste right now? You have just heightened your senses and increased the connection between your conscious and unconscious mind.

3. It Gathers and Sorts Information

In order to do the above exercise, you needed to slow your reading down slightly in order to process the suggestions, but no matter how fast or slow you were reading, the information was gathered and presented to you at the speed of thought—amazingly fast. The conscious mind *gathers* and *sorts* information, channeling it to the unconscious. At the same time, it deletes and distorts the information according to the language used in the transmission, along with any previously held beliefs that may have been present.

4. It Communicates with the Universal Consciousness (God) Through Your Unconscious Mind

The conscious mind has no direct link with the source of manifestation except by channeling through the unconscious mind, because to be understood and presented, words and ideas need to be translated into an interface of symbols or pictures. If the link between the conscious and unconscious is clear and strong, collaboration, and therefore manifestation, is easy. Low-energy emotions and nonsupportive beliefs serve to interfere with the energy flow, in effect cutting off the connection. High-energy emotions make the flow of energy amazingly easy.

5. It Tests Probabilities

Your conscious mind sorts out *probabilities*. If you decide to go out today, you will make a conscious decision about what to wear based on probabilities. If it's a beautiful, warm day you would most likely wear lightweight clothes.

6. It Is a Decision-Maker and a Judge

Your conscious mind may also decide to take a jacket, judging that it may get cooler in the evening, or extra money in case you decide to go to the movies later on.

7. It Presents Information to the Unconscious for Storage

As conclusions are reached, the conscious mind *presents the information to the unconscious mind* for it to store and commit to memory. Later in the evening of the example above, as you are wearing a lightweight jacket and the weather turns distinctly cold, you may store this information for the following evening, or even the following year, so that based on the new information received, the conscious mind can *retrieve information from the unconscious mind* and make a new decision to take a warmer jacket next time.

8. It Makes Generalizations

The conscious mind makes *generalizations*. As you stroll along, you may notice a cute animal. If it's got four legs, is furry, wags its tail, and barks, the conscious mind will conclude that it's probably a dog.

9. It Likes to Analyze and Categorize

Your conscious mind likes to *analyze and categorize*, both for the sake of efficiency and for protection, as it checks to find out if a pattern is to your benefit or not. However, the judgments that the conscious mind makes are only as good as the information retrieved from the storage unit of the unconscious mind, which may have filed away as many as a hundred and fifty thousand low-energy commands or warnings from parents or other authority figures before you reached the age of seven. These act as a strong filter, which your unconscious mind puts into place for what it believes to be your protection.

10. It Requests Information from the Unconscious Memory

Your conscious mind often uses will power to make you act, but given that only 10 percent of your mind is conscious, will power alone is not enough to help you to access the files, clear the filter, and succeed. If all it took was determination, we'd have all been successful long before now!

Up to 90 percent of your mind is *not* conscious, so no matter how much you *want* to change, if the unconscious mind is replaying old videos, DVDs or memories of when you did not succeed, your results may be inconsistent. If your thoughts and actions are to be effective, your unconscious mind, where the imagination lies, has to be in harmony, or agreement, with the conscious mind.

So how do you change the inner mind? The easiest way is to access and clear from the unconscious mind any outdated programming that it may hold in its storage files, replacing it with powerful new programming of clear intent and high motivation, so that the conscious and unconscious minds act in accord, forming a congruent understanding.

The more synchronization that takes place, the more quickly your desires become your reality as you access higher levels of consciousness. You will also find that by clearing your thoughts and language you become a clearer and more powerful conduit of encouragement and healing for both yourself and others in your life. You come to the realization that everything is possible.

The Private Life of Your Unconscious Mind

Why do you need to know how your unconscious mind works? *Because it controls 90 percent of your functioning and 100 percent of the successful results in your life.* The unconscious mind is essentially where we hold our awareness of anything other than conscious material.

You might think of the conscious mind as the computer operator. As the operator, you have complete control over what you program the computer to do. You decide what files to open and what files to keep, change, edit, or delete. You decide on the order of importance of documents and determine which documents are current, confidential, or to be filed. As the operator, sometimes you may have unremembered or mismatched files and sometimes the files have viruses that you are unaware of for now, although you do know that something is not quite right because the program isn't responding as quickly as it should.

Your unconscious mind has the most amazing possibilities when you learn how to use it. It is very much like the Internet, although most people use only a fraction of the Internet's capabilities. The mind's protective software is fantastic. It's programmed to filter, scan, clean, and heal viruses every second of every day. It will only be stopped from doing that if the operator continually overrides or overwrites its clear warning messages. It is a *servomechanism*: it acts only on your commands, unless preservation of the body is involved, at which point it will always attempt to override, or send a message to you. Your unconscious mind has no thoughts or feelings of its own; it gives results based on its authentic, original blueprint and the input of any subsequent programming by you.

Happy Outcomes

How can you get your unconscious mind to work with you toward some wonderful, happy outcomes? While the conscious mind can draw conclusions from what is not said or apparent, the unconscious mind can only produce results based on the accuracy of the question or the way information is presented to it by the conscious mind (the operator).

If you've ever tried to find a site on the Internet using key words, you'll understand how this system works. Type in the word "boxes" and you'll get anything from candy boxes to coffins. I was searching for an "alpha stimulator" and up popped all kinds of sex sites ("stimulate" can have other connotations than the meaning I had intended!). The unconscious mind also cannot differentiate between what is real and what is imaginary, just like the Internet.

Once you draw a conclusion consciously, or make a conscious decision, the unconscious mind stores that information in a file and gives future results based on that programming by the conscious mind. After that, no matter how much will power your conscious mind uses, over time the unconscious will eventually revert and present results based on previous programming. It's just like when you update a Word document and don't remember to save it; any new information is simply not accepted and the original file reappears. The file needs to be re-edited and saved by the conscious mind (by repetition of actions or language), or the unconscious mind needs to be convinced that health will increase or be compromised, in order for it to proceed differently.

The unconscious mind, which is also where manifestation begins, is made up of fundamental drives (genetic and collective) and memories. With repetition of actions or thought processes, habits are formed. Habits are useful in that they allow you not to have to reprocess every bit of the two million pieces of information that enter your brain *every second*. They enable you to make generalizations and expectations, rather like when you learn to drive a car—all the new information is a little much at first, but eventually driving becomes totally automatic. Driving an unfamiliar car takes just minutes to get used to because cars, although slightly different in their makeup, have generally the same format in the way that the brakes, steering wheels, wipers, and so forth work.

If we start to believe that a memory or habit is a fundamental drive, then that becomes our truth, and subsequently, our actualized reality. For example, by continually *choosing* relationships that are challenging, we may make the assumption that "all relationships are challenging" That becomes its own self-fulfilling prophecy and part of our belief system, and hence our reality.

When we add into the equation the fact that "reality" is totally subjective (ask three people to describe a dramatic or emotional occurrence and you may not think that they were talking about the same event), you have the likelihood of inconsistent results.

The bottom line for *successful* results is "right thinking": decisions made by repeating previous actions that turned out *well*. Before right thinking (and then right action) can occur, the first key to making changes happen is an increased awareness of your habits, self-talk, and suppositions. You can't change something that you don't know about!

The simple formula for change below will be expanded upon as we go through the book and do practical exercises that lead to ways you can turbo-boost and switch on all aspects of your life:

Awareness
plus
Availability of choice
(I always have a choice!)
leads to
Adaptation
(new ideas/creativity/learning)
to allow
Absorption/Assimilation
resulting in
Action
(*purposeful* action based on purposeful results)
leading to
Active participation in a great life!

So how do you first become aware of what the unconscious mind requires from you in order for it to supply your desires? You learn how it works. The good news is that you can reprogram the unconscious mind simply by understanding the instructions it needs in order to produce high-energy and directed output. The thoughts, words, pictures, sounds, and feelings you use to communicate with yourself shape what you perceive to be your reality. By consciously using words, you can consciously create the reality you want and deserve. You have at your fingertips, in the unconscious mind, an immense supply of previously untapped resources that are just a thought away.

As we go through the functions of the unconscious mind point by point, you may formulate different ideas about the way you speak and think for the future, so that your conscious and unconscious minds can begin to work together as a team or partnership. You will be amazed at how quickly a sense of peace and trust begins to grow in your life. You'll also be delighted by the way your desires become reality almost immediately, as you clear away previous patterns. Every small change that you notice will reinforce the belief that the work you are doing is paying off both emotionally and financially.

Quantum Mind Power—The Secret Treasure in Your Unconscious Mind

Your unconscious mind's blueprint is programmed to seek solutions as it moves toward integration and unity. It's designed to give you what you focus on. It acts on direct commands. It doesn't need you to be polite. While the conscious mind may need persuasion—"I'd really appreciate it if you'd open the window, please, because it's getting a little hot in here"—your unconscious prefers direct instruction: "Open the window now." You might think of it as a genie or a guardian angel, there to do your bidding. In order to comply, it needs the present tense (as in now) to induce action. You can make requests with a "please" and a "thank you," even though it's not a requirement, to raise the vibration of the instruction by using high-energy words. There are ten main things to understand about your unconscious mind:

1. Prime Directive: Your Health Is Truly Your Wealth

The unconscious mind's *number one* directive is to operate and preserve the physical body (survival), so *all* suggestions that have to do with keeping the body healthy are *immediately* accepted, remembered, and acted upon. Sometimes, it runs a program that it believes is for your protection, which you need to release and update in order to get better emotionally or physically.

For example, consider a child who feels unloved (love is a survival requirement for the human brain directive) or neglected. Because of this emotional "dis-ease," the child becomes physically unwell (all negative emotions eventually manifest physically), which then elicits the parents' love or attention that the child desires. The child's inner dialogue may then sound something like, "When I'm not well, I'm loved/safe," which the unconscious translates to mean that getting ill means survival. This pattern may continue into adulthood, at which point the unconscious mind's program needs to be revised: a child's (survival) needs and filters are not the same as an adult's, and as adults we have more choices and resources available to us to navigate our relationships.

To further build the communication link between your conscious and unconscious mind, just before you sleep at night you might want to direct your unconscious mind by saying to yourself, silently or aloud:

> *Please disconnect and release all negative emotions and limiting beliefs in the context of . . .* (whatever area is not working for you; the more specific the better) *NOW, while preserving all positive lessons for future use. Reconnect with the authentic blueprint of perfect health, wealth, and magical happiness, and bring me love, joy, great health, and abundance. Thank you.*

You can trust that your unconscious will respond—perhaps with an interesting dream, or you may have an unusual event the next day that gives you a clue about how you can become more connected with your unconscious mind. An open and curious attitude will go a long way to help you notice the signals.

The unconscious runs the body's autonomic nervous system, which includes respiration and breathing, the heart, the immune system, and digestion. Anything that keeps the body running efficiently is the domain of the unconscious mind.

You don't consciously know how to beat your heart any more than you know how to move your blood around your body or digest your food. However, your conscious thoughts can affect these smooth-running systems. Kinesiologists who use muscle testing have proven that low-energy thoughts produce weaker muscles, while high-energy (positive) thoughts generate stronger muscles.

A recent U.S. study of elderly people in bed with long-term disabilities proved that just *thinking* about exercising leg, arm, and body muscles for only ten minutes a day actually improved the muscle strength and appearance in less then a month. Your thoughts affect every cell in your body, so true healing takes place mentally *before* the physical healing occurs.

I recently used this health connection to stop a migraine. I have not had a migraine for many years, since I began using hypnosis. So as I awoke at 2:00 AM with that less than good feeling, which everyone who has ever had a migraine knows starts a three-day cycle, my first reaction was one of surprise. However, I knew that I had been putting in too many hours preparing for a big health show, so I sat up and said aloud:

I want to thank my unconscious mind now for reminding me that I have been overdoing it. I am listening and I am aware, and I'd like to tell you that in the best interest of my health, as I still have two days of work ahead, keep me healthy by letting go right now; help me to relax and sleep well tonight. Thank you.

I lay down (*without* taking any drugs). Ten minutes later my head was clear and I had a great sleep. By connecting with the idea of health, any suggestion will be acted upon with avid interest by the unconscious mind.

Be careful about how you talk to yourself—the word "diet" to the unconscious mind implies lack of food. Food is essential for the body to stay alive, so planning a diet will most likely result in many trips to the fridge to stock up. Suggesting instead, *I love to eat fruit and vegetables now because fresh food makes me slimmer and therefore healthier,* is a much better way to persuade the unconscious mind to join in the quest for slimness.

Could you find ways to get rich by using the health connection in the words you speak to yourself? How about using this powerful statement: *I am rich and wealthy now because prosperity allows me to relax more and so become healthier!*

Be as inventive and imaginative as you can; your unconscious *loves* suggestions that are given in a fun way because they keep the conscious mind occupied and out of the way while the unconscious is doing its job of making changes.

2. The Unconscious Mind Has a Direct Connection with the Universal Mind, or God

Edgar Cayce, known as the Sleeping Prophet, used to say that the use of "imaginative forces" is the key to spiritual awareness. The altered states produced by hypnosis, prayer, meditation, or simply the use of imagination open a doorway and direct connection to the higher self and higher power. The results, in what appear to be "miracles," will actually become commonplace occurrences the more we learn to utilize the dynamic energy of the unconscious mind.

3. It Stores and Organizes Memories

The unconscious mind remembers everything, which is a very useful tool if used in a directed way. I remember an experience with my father when I was fourteen years old. He had a burning pan of fat and was walking toward the back door, his hands burning as the flames got higher and higher with the fresh oxygen from the doorway. Without thinking I grabbed a tea towel, soaked it in water, and threw it on the pan, dousing the flames immediately. I have no recollection of when or where I learned that trick, but we were both very glad that my unconscious mind had the memory somewhere and had stored it for later use.

Inside your head is your brain, a mechanism so amazing that it filters, sorts, and processes two million pieces of information every second. It sorts the information into chunks of 126 (more or less), and then presents them for storage and filing in groups of seven (plus or minus two). This is why we use phone numbers in groups of seven numbers—they're much easier to remember. During the sorting process the information is generalized before it is stored and filed, sometimes becoming distorted or deleted. A current experience may trigger a memory and a response then takes place, using the recalled memory as a conscious means to judge what the appropriate action should be. If the memory is stored efficiently, and no distortion occurs, then the result is as easy as remembering how to ride a bike. However, if *emotions* are involved in the storage or retrieval of a memory, unexpected outcomes can occur.

4. It Stores and Operates Our Emotions

Emotions are stored and operated from within the unconscious mind. Sometimes, negative emotions and the events surrounding them are suppressed from conscious awareness until a later event or memory activates that emotion. The unconscious mind then presents the suppressed emotion again in order for the conscious mind to resolve it.

Emotions are at the root of our behavior. They are the driving force behind motivation and behind any decision to take action (people generally move *toward* pleasure and *away from* pain). Emotions stored in the unconscious are the most powerful ones, as they surface when "triggered" by an immediate event. Both pleasurable and not so pleasant current experiences can trigger previous memories.

The role of the unconscious mind is to present and manifest the emotion that is most appropriate to what is happening in the current event or experience. However, if an event is strong or overpowering, the correct emotional response may not immediately register, as the "fight-or-flight" survival mechanism kicks in. If the unconscious mind feels that survival may be compromised, or some kind of threat is imminent, or even if the emotional response is simply too much (as in grief at the death of a loved one), then the unconscious mind may put appropriate emotions to one side and store them in order for the person to just "get by." Dissociation (apparent lessening, or even complete lack, of feeling) is the result, which is an excellent *temporary* protective mechanism. Later, these stored emotions may get triggered at an appropriate (or inappropriate) time, as the unconscious mind will take any and every opportunity to release these unwanted memories.

"Forgotten" memories can surface in the form of impulses and compulsions; we may not even know why we act as we do because the memory that triggered the compulsion is still hidden. For example, food can have emotional ties to comfort or love, which can trigger overeating to stimulate endorphins in order to keep us "balanced." However, overeating or less healthy eating leads to even further physical and emotional imbalance, and a cycle, or loop, is created.

5. It Maintains Genealogical Instincts

The fight-or-flight survival mechanism is an instinctual memory that is a response to stress. It's hardwired into our neurology and is primarily a protective device. Our ancestors needed to respond to a surprise attack by either fleeing or fighting, both of which require a burst of energy in the body to provide a means for survival. Anything instinctive is usually a genetic memory: eating, sleeping, reproduction, and glandular function are just a few of the instinctive patterns that allow us to lead more efficient lives.

Unconscious thought processes, which served a useful purpose, were stored and utilized in the form of impulses. For example, food cravings are an instinctive need of the body, which used to be vital thousands of years ago, when our ancestors had the task of hunting for their food and then had to prepare or cook it before the craving could be satisfied.

These days, we in the Western world have no real need for cravings, as food is almost always available. When we are aware of the need to eat, we go to the fridge or cupboard and eat. Even before the craving is satisfied (usually in around two or three minutes) we have already taken steps to satisfy it.

6. It Creates and Maintains Least-Effort Patterns

Habitual behavior is easily established. Once learned, you can comfortably direct your attention elsewhere and just run the program. Driving a car is a perfect example of this. By automatically knowing how to *mechanically* drive a car, the conscious mind is freed, ready to instantly learn any new information presented in the way of unusual road conditions or other drivers' behavior.

We call all these habitual behavior patterns "routines" and a routine is a useful, easy pattern to establish, with obvious constructive benefits. An example of an *unfavorable* routine is that of the instant gratification of snacking while watching television, or staying in a job just because it is "comfortable." This behavior can be changed by a powerful push from the unconscious mind. Studies show that it takes a mere twenty-one days to establish a new behavior pattern or habit. A habit is an acquired behavior that is repeated until it becomes almost involuntary. There's a tendency to think of habits as unfavorable. In fact, *beneficial habits are just as easy to establish as unfavorable ones.*

7. It Communicates With Symbols

The unconscious uses the language of metaphor and imagination to create the future, in partnership with the conscious mind.

Your thoughts begin with words that you use to represent your desires to your unconscious mind. It translates these into imagery and presents information back to you in the form of metaphors or symbols. Each individual forms a model or map of the world, which is used to guide behavior. Being purely subjective, every choice we take makes sense when viewed in the context of our own model. If we are to understand our experiences, then these models will guide us.

Sometimes these models do not serve us. They may become less flexible, leading to incorrect choices being made, or they may become uncreative, leading to *no* choices being made. To greatly expand your own growth-producing choices, you simply switch your self-talk, increase your imagery and imagination, and formulate clear intentions followed by immediate action.

8. It Takes Direction from the Conscious Mind

The unconscious mind will only accept suggestions from someone it respects—which could be why your unconscious mind doesn't always listen to you.

How is your unconscious mind possibly going to want to follow your suggestions unless you love and respect yourself? The unconscious mind believes about you what you believe about yourself (as do other people). Your self-worth is truly the foundation for your beliefs and the manifestation of a great self-image, success, and happiness.

How many times have you praised yourself today? How many rewards or gifts have you given yourself? How do you talk about yourself? Which reminds me—how do you talk about *other* people?

9. It Accepts Things Literally and Personally

Be careful what you say about other people: your unconscious mind thinks you're talking about *yourself*, because it responds only to the key words you use, not realizing that you are talking about someone else! Your self-worth may be less great than it could be because your inner mind accepts all your words as the truth. One way to change this is by switching your key words.

10. It Does Not Process Negative Commands

Do *not* think of a white elephant. Do *not* think of a white elephant with pink spots—dancing on a stage. Do *not* remember the number 167. Which number are you not to remember? Your unconscious cannot process what is *not*. It simply responds to the key words you give it. Children under seven are inclined to respond like the unconscious mind. Tell a child "Don't touch that!" and notice what response you get.

As you read the following words, notice how you are feeling:

And now, just thinking about all the tension and tightness in your shoulders, all the day-to-day worries and concerns, relax your shoulders and just let them go.

Where is your imagination right now? Alternatively, notice what you are feeling as you read this:

And now, just thinking about your shoulders, relaxing them, releasing and imagining a beautiful pink energy like liquid light flowing down and through the shoulders, softly, softly letting go ... o ... o.

You may want to be aware of the difference that words can have by remembering these two examples as you speak to other people in your daily life.

Your unconscious mind is like the Internet, which recognizes and processes the key words in a sentence and responds by reminding you of all the other chains of words, memories, and meanings stimulated by each key word (including genetic and past life memories). Negative words have been proven to produce lower (heavier) vibration or energy, and positive words produce a higher (lighter) vibration or energy. You even feel "heavy" when you are aware of low-energy emotions and "light" when you feel good.

I hear people every day saying, "No problem!" when they really mean "You're welcome" or "I'm happy to do that." Just think what the unconscious mind actually hears. It doesn't process the "no" and so it just hears "problem." Go ahead and do your own Internet searches. Your unconscious mind is a billion times more powerful than any computer yet invented. How many chains of meaning, memories, or events were triggered by that one word? In fact, by changing the low-energy key words to high-energy ones, you can actually change your mind! For example:

- "It's hard" becomes *"It's not easy."*
- "I'm broke" becomes *"I'm not rich."*
- "I'm afraid" becomes *"I have no courage."*
- "I'm sick" becomes *"I'm not very healthy."*

Switching your language provides a wonderful solution for stopping nonproductive inner talk. Observe how the unconscious mind hears those sentences:

- "It's (not) easy."
- "I'm (not) rich."
- "I have (no) courage."
- "I'm (not) very healthy."

Change Your Language, Change Your Destiny

How does becoming aware and changing your language impact your life? Let me give you a few examples:

Kirsten, a yoga teacher and client, had this to report:

I've chosen my words so much more carefully this last week. During a private yoga class, I was able to repeatedly correct and make my student aware of the constant flow of limiting and negative commentary she had about herself. She was so grateful because she wasn't even aware of how often those thoughts came up!

Elaine is someone I've known for many years. A well-known graphologist and handwriting analyst, always on the go and a real mover and a shaker in most areas of her life, she had been resisting buying her own home, coming up with plenty of reasons why she couldn't get the down payment. Using the tools for switching her thoughts and language changed her experience dramatically:

Transforming words such as "problem" and "bad" into "opportunity," "challenge," "exciting," and similar words has helped me transform my speech and my way of thinking. By becoming aware of my own language patterns and changing them, I am finding life so much easier, and my prosperity has increased to the point where I recently put a deposit on a condo, which I am already well on the way to being able to buy with cash by the time it is built.

Joanne, a training consultant and company owner, came to me to certify as a hypnotherapist to increase her skill set. During my seven-day training, we play a game. Each individual gets twenty coins on the first day. Participants are told that if they use a low-energy word, they will forfeit a coin to the person who catches them. The catcher says, "Switch!" and the person who's been caught must replace the low-energy word with a high-energy word or phrase. If a person catches him or herself before the other person catches them (for instance, they might say: "It's hard . . . Oops! Rather, it's not easy!"), they can claim a coin from the other person, thus encouraging everyone to be aware of the words they are using. All the participants without exception begin on the first day by insisting that they are positive talkers and thinkers and so don't need to play!

Joanne did not like this game at all and wanted to quit after the first two days. As a talker and trainer, she spends her life talking to people and asking questions. During the game, however, she didn't want to speak because she could not keep her coins once she opened her mouth! She told me that she quickly learned from the exercise that she doesn't speak positively at all, and that she was frequently using negative words. She realized that there were many times when people misunderstood what she said or meant because of her negative language.

On the second week, she told another student that she had lost her voice since playing the game, figuratively speaking. Amazingly, she really did lose her voice from laryngitis, which came on suddenly as she was flying to Vancouver to conduct a training of her own. Throughout the three days of the training she continually spoke to herself about how well she felt, and how clear her voice was, to ensure that she could finish the training. It worked.

Joanne wrote to thank me, saying,

It's amazing how switching my language and my thoughts has had such an impact on my life, both for myself, concerning my health and my interaction with family and business associates, and my customers. I'm so much more positive as a result.

Wilma took her training at the same seminar as Joanne. Just before the course, she was diagnosed with cancer. It manifested behind her right eye, and she was in a great deal of pain when she arrived on the first day. The second day as she walked in, I asked her how she was feeling. "I'm feeling blessed. Lucky to have found you and this class when I needed so much support." The following day her only comment was: "I had an interesting night."

I admired her so much because she kept on going, one eye closed, grateful for everyone and everything. We all hugged her at the end of each day because she was such an inspiration. Today, Wilma is back home with her family in Barbados. She credits her amazing resilience to God and the positive thinking and speaking techniques she learned with us.

> *If you realized how powerful your thoughts are,*
> *you would never think a negative thought.*
> —Mildred Norman Ryder,
> a.k.a. *Peace Pilgrim* (1908–1981)

Magic of the Mind

At the beginning of the book, I promised you that I would teach you a great Magic of the Mind state that allows you to access your unconscious and higher mind to go into the state of instant optimism. You're about to learn it. In chapter two you learned about self-worth, which is why this Magic of the Mind exercise works and is so effective. In chapter five you'll learn how to clear and release negative emotions completely in one minute, using an extension of this magical state. It's something that you can teach to children or students, and it's also called the Learning State. It's wonderful to use in the classroom or lecture hall; all learning is unconscious, so any new information is absorbed and integrated much more quickly. In this state you can only access high-energy emotions, so you can make anxiety a thing of the past!

You can do Magic of the Mind Three anywhere—on a bus, at traffic lights, in a classroom, at a business meeting, at the dentist to calm you down, or just before a job interview. When you use it just before an interview (go into this state and stay in it while you are being interviewed), you'll stay in control and feel amazingly confident.

Magic of the Mind Three

As you sit comfortably with your back straight, allow your head to remain facing forward with your chin slightly up. Raise your eyes to ceiling level. Find a place where the ceiling meets the wall and simply stare at this spot.

Now become aware of what's to your right and what's to your left, without moving your eyes or head. To make sure you are doing this, stretch out your arms from your sides and lift them to the level of your head, with your palms facing out (you should be able to see the backs of your hands at eye level), and wiggle your fingers while drawing your hands back toward your ears so that you can only just see them. Now drop them into your lap and remain aware of what you can see in your peripheral vision.

At this point you'll start to feel very relaxed, and you'll become aware that your breathing is slowing down. If you wish, you can increase the feel-good factor by thinking of a wonderful, safe place in nature.

Now adjust your eyes to normal level, still using that peripheral vision, and go about your daily life. If you are in a seminar or class, you can still be aware of what's on either side of you as you look at and listen to the teacher or trainer. Your learning will be dramatically improved. This magical state is perfect to use while you're driving; you have a much wider vision and are much more aware of traffic coming up behind you and to the side.

From now on, every time you remember, go into this state and simply go about your normal life. You'll be surprised by how much more calm and in control you feel each day as you learn to access your unconscious mind at will.

Recap

Your Conscious Mind:

1. Is aware of what it perceives
2. Is in contact with reality through the sense organs—touch, sight, hearing, smell, and taste

3. Gathers and sorts out information in order to send it to the unconscious mind
4. Can communicate with the universal consciousness or super consciousness (God/Universal Mind) *only* through the unconscious mind—*it has no direct link when low-energy thoughts or limiting beliefs are present*
5. Tests probabilities in order to decide what action to take; it can think deductively (you think something)
6. Is a decision-maker and a judge
7. Reviews and evaluates information, draws conclusions, and presents those conclusions to the unconscious mind for storage
8. Makes generalizations; it can think inductively (makes you think)
9. Likes to analyze and categorize
10. Requests information from the unconscious memory, often from deep inside; will power alone is not enough to change the information

Your Unconscious Mind:

1. Operates and preserves the health of the physical body (*prime directive*)
2. Has a *direct* connection with the super consciousness/collective unconscious/God/universal consciousness
3. Stores and organizes memories—it remembers *everything*
4. Stores emotions in the physical body (suppressing strong low-energy emotions to present to the conscious mind to resolve at a later date)
5. Maintains genealogical instincts
6. Creates and maintains least-effort patterns
7. Uses metaphor and imagination to create the future in partnership with the conscious mind—communicates with symbols
8. Takes direction from the conscious mind—will only accept suggestions from someone it *respects*
9. Accepts things literally and personally
10. Does not process negative commands

Chapter Three Action Plan

1. Switch! Ask friends or family to let you know of the one negative word or phrase you use most often, and work on switching that one every day until it's cleared from your vocabulary.
2. Listen to the key words that other people use when you're at the supermarket or bank.
3. Make a note of any emotions that you feel tomorrow—both negative and positive. Which word or feeling comes up most often for you?
4. Go into the Magic of the Mind Three state every day for fifteen minutes until it becomes natural for you to be in it constantly.
5. Review the list of low-energy words in the appendix and clear them from your language.

You are now aware of some of the reasons why things don't always turn out the way you want them to. You are also beginning to understand how you can actively switch on your inner dialogue to gain control of your life and emotions. Your words are gifts that you give and receive. You have the power today to make someone (including yourself) feel much better about life and themselves.

Let's move on now and find out more about what you can do to open up your world!

4

The Power of Focus and Intention

When skiing downhill on an icy day, keep your shoulders facing toward your destination and look for the snow.

Leap into Life—and Love It!

I first learned to ski when I went to Austria in my late twenties. The instructor was taking a group of about ten of us down a very icy slope. We were all beginners, and we had to learn on intermediate slopes because there was not much snow around. The *real* learners' slopes were barely covered.

The instructor's cries of "Mind zee ice!" rang in my ears as I side-slipped to negotiate the mountainside. Sure enough, as soon as I saw the ice, I landed on my bottom. Nevertheless, I enjoyed the experience; I was even quite proud of all the bruises. However, every time I went skiing after that, I would bump my way down to the bottom of every slope, usually more on my rear end than on the skis. I just figured that I must be more daring than the others. This went on every year until one year when I was skiing with friends and I watched one of the men go easily down the same slope that I had just tumbled down. I asked him, "What's the secret? How do you avoid the ice?" "I look for the snow!" he replied. It sounds so easy when it's put like that, doesn't it?

What do you dream of being? What do you dream of doing with your life? Do you have a clear idea of what you want? What is it that you're looking forward to? It's in speaking your dreams that you breathe life into them and they become reality. You are the guardian of your happiness. It's time to believe in amazing possibilities because possibilities make you care about the future. They inspire hope, and hope is always replenishing and uplifting.

The second you took your first breath, you had the potential to be great, and true greatness is measured by your ability to follow your desires with strong energy, clear intent, and a powerful, trusting leap into the future. Passion, high-energy words, and conviction open the door to your new destiny. The truth of your character is determined by the vastness of your dreams, and successful results are determined by the strength of the connection you have with yourself and your inner mind. It really doesn't matter if your goals are simple or involved as long as you spend every day living really well. The life you are living right now is the result of everything you've thought or believed for years. As Frederick Langbridge, a British writer and priest from the end of the nineteenth century, said: "Two men look out through the same bars; one sees the mud and one the stars."

Many people don't know exactly what they want or why they want it, but they're busy working as hard as they can to get it! They are busy building bridges that aren't needed because there are no rivers to cross. Their unconscious minds are out there playing in the stars because they are not sending out a clear, directed signal. So how do you know if you're on track with sending out your desires? When you set a goal with a high intent, your unconscious mind will automatically let you know if your wants and needs are in alignment by sending you messengers.

Your Emotions

Twenty percent of the words you use are emotional impact words. Half of that 20 percent are negative, or low-energy, and half are high-energy. That means that you always have the choice of which to use to bring you high-energy returns. Actually, you already have all the answers as you begin to think and speak yourself happy now.

The simple truth is that if you meet the real experiences of life with intelligence and curiosity, negative emotions or events become feedback that you can view with interest while asking yourself what lesson is to be learned—or what more you need to know—in order to succeed. Get ready to set new goals with clarity, energy, and determination. Commit to achieving your goals, and have faith in tomorrow.

Before we begin to get you everything you want, I'd like you to do something: get a pen and a blank sheet of paper, and get ready to write down your goals. Or open a new document on your computer. Do this now, please. It's important because we're about to do an exercise that I want you to do without knowing the answers up front. The blank page is there to remind you that you have the freedom to fill out your future like a blank check. Writing goals with your hand is also one of the most concrete ways to start them manifesting, because your mind is directly connected to your body and recording physically anchors them into your unconscious storage files. It also gets you used to taking action before you think—another important success strategy.

Action is the bridge between dreams and reality. It may be uncomfortable for a while, but it's not always comfortable when you're growing, so welcome that feeling. Are you willing to create your abundant life now? Do you want a better job or a purpose that adds value to your life and to the lives of others? Are you ready to be rich and happy? You know how to succeed. You've already been successful at something in your life.

Rich and successful people are exactly like you, except that they have a different strategy. They plan and then commit to their plan with the expectation of success, ready to change and adjust as they go. Successful people make "mistakes" often, and use them as feedback to show them what they need to know that they wouldn't have known otherwise. In fact, the more quickly and often you go the incorrect way, the faster you can achieve outstanding results! Almost everything you want to do or have has been done or had by someone before. Model someone who's already achieved it with excellence and then take it up a notch.

You already know that all behavior, learning, and change occur first at the unconscious level and then you become aware of them at a conscious level. Change, however, is not the end but the journey. It's a journey from a not very satisfactory present state toward a more pleasant desired state or outcome. Change simply for the sake of it merely stirs energy around, rather like throwing a pebble in a pond. To really make things happen, it's important to set your course toward a specific goal or place. Add in excitement and anticipation and you speed up your results like a rocket booster. Anxiety, by the way, is simply your unconscious mind's way of letting you know that you need to focus more specifically on what you want.

What *Do* You Really Want?

What is the one thing you've promised yourself for as long as you can remember? Now is the time to make a date and start planning it. Get ready to focus exclusively on what you want, every minute of every day, to bring your success.

Let's open up your imagination so that the unconscious mind can zoom out to get you all your answers. Happiness begins in the realm of your imagination, and imagination is absolutely necessary for perception; so to perceive your future all you have to do is imagine it! What would you be or do if you could have anything you wanted? Get your paper ready, and do the following exercise (with each dollar amount on a separate page) to find out your hidden desires:

Reach for the Stars—Rich and Loving It!

I have $1,000,000 ... today ... tax free!

I buy _____

Length of time I take off work is _____

The new work I do is _____

I learn _____

The people I give money to are _____ and the amount is $ _____

The charity I donate to is _____ and the amount is $ _____
I invest $ _____ in stocks/stores/property/other (specify) _____
Benefits of having this amount _____

I have $5,000,000 ... today ... tax free!

I buy _____
(assuming that I'd bought all the previous things already)
Length of time I take off work is _____
The new work I do is _____
I learn _____
The people I give money to are _____ and the amount is $_____
The charity I donate to is _____ and the amount is $ _____
I invest $ _____ in stocks/stores/property/other (specify) _____
Benefits of having this amount _____

I have $1 billion ... today ... tax free!

I buy _____
(assuming that I'd bought all the previous things already)
Length of time I take off work is _____
The new work I do is _____
I learn _____
The people I give money to are _____ and the amount is $_____
The charity I donate to is _____ and the amount is $ _____
I invest $ _____ in stocks/stores/property/other (specify) _____
Benefits of having this amount _____

Results:

Everything you wrote on the $1,000,000 page is totally within reach. Act on everything, and initially bump each one down a little to begin manifesting right now.

Example:
I buy: *two new houses and a new car*
(One house and change my car)

Time off work: *forever!*
(Change my job now!)

Time off work: *six months*
(Find a great hobby)

The new work:
(Start researching courses to prepare for it)

I learn:
(Start saving *now* and decide the earliest date you can
begin)

The people I give money to:
(Do something nice for everyone you wrote down here: a
shopping trip, a nice compliment, a bunch of flowers, etc.)

The charity:
(Give a small amount to the same charity)

Investment:
(Open a small savings account or take out an endowment
or insurance policy)

On the $5,000,000 page, you wrote down the possibilities
within the next five years, and on the $1 billion page, you wrote
down your ultimate goal in life (if you couldn't think of anything,
by the way, then start imagining!). Now make a contract with
yourself following the sample on the next page.

Money, love, wealth, health, and happiness are like air—there is
more than enough for everybody for as long as they live. As you
wake up in the morning, do you ever think about how much air
there is to breathe today? There's no reason to because you know
that there's more than enough. When you believe that there is
always going to be more than enough money, love, and happiness,
it becomes a self-fulfilling prophecy. The very fact that you can
imagine yourself in a happy, successful situation means that it is
well within your reach.

Success means so many different things to so many different
people that *you* need to be able to decide what's really important

My Promise:

I promise myself NOW to give 100 percent commitment to all my goals. I am ready to direct and star in the masterpiece that is my life, as I welcome change with the excitement and wonder of the five-year-old child I still am inside.

I promise myself to celebrate just being me as I surrender to the greater wisdom I have inside, and connect with the source of the wellspring of life: a joyous reuniting with spirit.

I view myself and others with compassion and forgiveness as I open all doors and windows to endless possibilities for success and happiness. I recognize and thank myself for having the courage and strength to come this far. I also give thanks for every lesson because each one reveals more of the real me.

Any time I am less than passionate about life I remember to look for the beauty as I view ALL events as opportunities for growth.

I promise to follow my inner light—the light that connects me to myself and others. Today's goal is: to have fun relaxing.

My short-term goals (within one week) are (list three):

My next month's goals are (list three):

My long-term goals (within five years—list three) are:

Right now I am in the most powerful moment of my life. This is the ONLY time I can start the change as I feel the excitement inside that brings me to health, love, happiness, and wealth. I am home.

Signed: Date:

to you. What do you want? Is it money? Prestige? Happy relationships? All of these? You need to know *why* you want changes to happen and be able to state your intent. Do you just want to change your job or do you need to change your whole career? Do you want a nice relationship or do you really want love, marriage, and a family?

Success happens when you feel fulfilled, complete, and at ease. At the end of the day, success is not how much stuff you accumulate or how slim you are. Real success is based on peace of mind, on how people remember you, and on how happy you make yourself and others. When I asked the children in my daughter's class (eleven-year-olds) what was important in life, they only came up with three things: home, play, and family. Did you notice as you did the exercise on what you really wanted that, as you realized that all your wants were fulfilled (three houses, ten cars, a private plane, etc.), your thoughts started to turn toward making a lasting foundation for the future? Perhaps something that you could contribute toward that would make a difference to humanity?

What you believe to be true becomes your truth. Look for the good in everyone and everything, and you'll find it. Search for sameness, not differences. Life is easy when you focus on what you want and take action to get it. You are the complete master of your destiny, so get ready to focus on what you really want. You now know that your unconscious mind is a vast sea of knowledge, like the Internet. New knowledge is out there all the time, but unless you sit down, turn on the computer, and make the connection, you may not even be aware of the mass of information available to help you find solutions to become successful and happy.

You can easily make the connection to success through your own *inner* Internet if you clearly say or think your intention in dynamic words that state what you want. By acting powerfully, with strong interest in the results you get, you'll become more flexible and keep on finding new and better solutions

Goal-Setting for Fast Results

Goal clarity is your gateway to the stars. Your unconscious relies on the words you use, with both yourself and others, to understand what you want as your intention. So if you think about clearing debt, you'll get lots more of it. Think about making money, and you'll get more of that. Asking yourself some very important questions makes you really focus on the specifics, and the more specific you get, the more easily and quickly you attain results. We're going to begin by writing down one simple thing that you want. Go ahead and do that now. The plan is to take one small action toward your goal within an hour. Then we're going to up the action to bigger and better things. However big or small the goal, follow this process: *Motivation, Intention, Action, Expectation, Flexibility, and Gratitude.*

Motivation

Ask yourself why: For what specific purpose? For what intent do I want this? Because I want (to be, do, or have).... Make sure your motivation is moving positively toward your goal, not away from it. Please be aware that "Because I don't want..." is an "away from" motivation. It's like driving by looking in the rear view mirror.

Intention

What exactly do you intend the results to be? For this question, answer some others:

- *How* much of it do I want of it, specifically?
- *What* can I do with it when I get it?
- *What* satisfaction does it give me?
- *When* do I expect to achieve this (exact date within the year)?
- *Who* is with me? Is it for me only?

Action

Answer these questions:

- *How* do I begin? *What's* the very first step?
- *When* do I start? *What* specific action can I take to start today?

Expectation

Desire, enthusiasm, and dynamic expectation are how you experience the excitement that takes you on a turbo-boost ride to success. Strong emotion catches the eye of both your unconscious mind and God. The happier the accompanying emotion, the faster and better the results. Ask yourself, *how much* do I want it? Is the answer so-so, I really want it, or I want it so much I can almost taste it? I live it, breathe it and focus on how I can achieve it every day. I'm always thinking of new, better, and fun ways to make it happen.

You know the correct answer, of course. Keep your dreams alive with fun and laughter. When dreams become too much work, they become colorless and momentum slows. Ask yourself these questions:

- *How* do I know when I've got it? This is something real: a ring, a plane ride, a baby in my arms. "I'll feel good" is not specific enough.
- *What* emotional satisfaction does it bring me?
- *What's* the emotional word that lights me up inside? Is it joy, excitement, exuberance, or a feeling of *I did it!*? Be exact.
- *What* makes it exciting? Is it a sound, a color, a feeling, a sensation, a smell, a taste?
- *What* else is exciting about it?

Flexibility

Winners find the easy way and change often. Small actions accomplish every task more quickly, so for every level of the process, make a plan to take as many small steps as possible (one phone call, one new outfit, one hour of healthy eating). Add in more steps as you go for greater choice.

How many steps do I take to get there?

The first number that comes into my head is ... ? Write out each step.

I worked with children at a special education school in South Africa where the five- to nine-year-olds were diagnosed as being extremely uncoordinated and having very little attention span. They were assigned a teacher one on one, who taught and watched them, making a written minute-by-minute report to calibrate how long the children were able to concentrate as they were being treated. The treatments included crawling around the gym on hands and knees to increase coordination, and fun exercises with drawing and copying. It was amazing how much change occurred in just one week. The teachers kept records of their progress and discovered by close observation that the children were able to focus twice as much with the individual attention—two minutes instead of one minute, in some cases. The praise the children received brought dramatic improvements, and many of them were exhibiting normal ranges of attention and behavior within six months.

Gratitude

Gratitude expands your success exponentially because all gratitude is high-energy emotion. Every day, write in a gratitude book or day planner how grateful you are for the good *and* the not so good. The not so good is simply pointing out where more thought and action is necessary. So view any obstacle as good news that you're moving forward. Watch out for old patterns emerging, and change them as you go.

How quickly does this goal-setting work? If you've made the goal specific enough with clear words and powerful emotions, you'll see results in less than a day. How do you know? You'll simply feel good and more hopeful about life. You'll find yourself planning to do something fun, because when your unconscious mind is clear about the instruction, it will encourage you to go and play while it does the work of bringing home your results.

Word Empowerment

Christl took the seven-day training I taught on word empowerment called "Change Your Words, Change Your World." She sent me an email three weeks later:

> *"Change your Words, Change your World"* made a compelling case for me to lead a happy and healthy life with the easy formula of changing speech habits from negative to positive. The result? I am calmer. My mind is paying less attention to worst-case scenarios, which I used to mull over endlessly. They've gone with the

negative-speak. In fact, the exercise has forced me to live in the moment, the Now, to help me pay attention to what I am saying. It's been amazing how more colorful the flowers in my garden have become; how time with my Mom has become more meaningful. I listen better to my friends. I'm having a great time.

So, are you ready for the big goal? Make this next goal so huge that when you get it, you'll know that this is the best book you ever read! Simply make the timeline a little longer, so that your unconscious mind can harness the power you're sending out. Dare yourself to stretch.

The Random Factor

Let's make it more interesting by consciously planting suggestions into your future and letting your unconscious mind decide what it wants you to notice. In your day planner, quickly choose four or five days in the next month. Simply mark them. Then on the days you've chosen, write at the top something such as: "Great day!" or "Wow day!" or "Happy day!" "This is the day I get great news! A happy letter, phone call, or message today."

Make up some phrases that really get you upbeat. Once a day for the whole month, flick through and read the comments, and truly wonder what's going to happen. Sometimes, in the beginning stages of doing this, you'll get the answer a day later, but the more you practice, the more clarity and accuracy you'll have in your manifestations.

Visualization: The Power of Your Mind

The power of thought is *amazing*. A number of years ago, I really needed to sell a house that I'd renovated with my ex-boyfriend. The money we didn't have was mounting, along with low-energy feelings. The house, a beautiful Victorian barn with a cathedral gallery, stained glass windows, crown molding, and endless detail, had been on the market since October with hardly any interest. It was now February (in cold, wet, rainy England). I sat down one day and decided to come up with a "sell by" date. It was the last possible date that I would want to be out of the house. I created a picture in my mind of a letter saying "Congratulations! You have sold 'The Stables' for more than the asking price." The date at the top of the letter was Sunday, May 22.

March came and went. Easter came with still no luck. We changed realtors, and every time I saw the "For Sale" sign I visualized my little scenario with the letter and imagined SOLD written across the notice board.

A stream of people came through the house, but no takers. Finally, one weekend in May a flurry of visitors arrived. One man walked in, shook my hand, and said, "I'll offer you the full asking price—I love it. I'm going straight to the real estate office to sign the deal." I was thrilled. "Quick, what date is it?" I asked my ex-boyfriend. "May twenty-first," he answered. "Hey, quite good!" I said. "A day early!"

The next day, first thing, another man arrived to say that he also loved the house. "Someone has already offered us the full price," I told him.

"I'll give you more than the asking price," he said, "and I want to move in by the first of June," only nine days away. It was the twenty-second of May! By the way, the original offer from the other man didn't happen. He apparently never even went into the real estate agent's office.

Did I engineer that date and price? Did I pick up something from the future, or did I plant the thought for the future? What does it matter? The fact is that high-energy visualization really does work. Your unconscious mind thinks in imagination and pictures and when you see it, feel it, breathe it, taste it, touch it, smell it, and hear it, your mind truly believes your visualization to be reality and will lead you right to it. You can dip into the future and "remember" future events. The way to make it easier for yourself is to ensure that visualizations and goals are *intense, realistic, and big,* with a date and time that are believable to your conscious mind. Use your amazing, innate creative intelligence to create excellence and magic.

Magic of the Mind Four

Future Dipping

You can do these exercises mentally as you read, or record the scripts and then visualize as intensely as you possibly can.

Imagine that you are in your own private theater, ready to watch a film that you're directing. Make the theater as comfortable as you can (plush chairs or sofas, luxurious carpet—you make it up). The screen is in front of you. Use the remote control in your hand to turn down the lights and begin the show.

First, imagine observing on the screen flashes of the *prequel* of your own life in black and white. Make this a really fun beginning. You may hear a voice say,

"And here it is: _____'s (your name) life so far!" Quick clips follow of previous episodes in your life. Of course, like any great film, it has drama and excitement (*pause*). Then listen as the voice asks, "What was learned? (*pause*) What was achieved? (*pause*) Is it time to move on now? What does the future hold? Stay with us as we look ahead now." Suddenly, you observe yourself on the screen, laughing, looking happy and healthy, living in a wonderful space with people you love, working at something you love to do that brings you pleasure and benefits others.

A date appears at the top right-hand corner of the screen. It's a day and a month in the near future, in the current year. It flashes on and off vividly. You notice that the program in your hand has the same date.

Feel yourself being drawn into the screen. You know: when you get so absorbed in a movie that it feels like you're there, looking through your own eyes. Who is there with you, or are you alone? Brighten up the colors and feel what you can feel, hear what you can hear. Touch and smell and taste the moment as you tingle with excitement. Where is that feeling in your body? Is there movement in the film or is it more like a snapshot? Does it feel like freedom or fun or both? Stay there until it really feels like a solid experience.

Close your eyes and find yourself back in the theater, observing yourself happy and alive on the screen. Take a deep breath of satisfaction and smile inside. Just before the film ends, what's the last thing that has to happen to make you feel that the story has a happy ending?

You may find yourself listening to people clapping with delight because it's such a great film. As the lights go up you may observe people congratulating you, patting you on the back, or shaking your hand.

Magic of the Mind Five

For this future event, decide on the time you want the event to occur. Remember to write an *exact* time—the day, month, and year. Close your eyes. Now imagine seeing yourself in a normal setting. Watch yourself as you pick up a letter from the mailbox.

Find yourself looking through your own eyes. Open the letter and "pan in" the camera for a close-up.

Again, observe the date at the top of the letter. Then: "Congratulations!

"You, _____, (your name) have done it!

"You _____ (here you will write the event)!" For example:

You won the lottery!
You sold your house!
You are engaged to the most wonderful person!
You overcame all and were pronounced fit and healthy!
You got the job!

Imagine the scene unfolding as you dissociate from the picture, floating above it and observing yourself laughing and smiling as you move into your new house; imagine yourself on your wedding day, surrounded by your friends and family, or see yourself shaking hands as you are offered that great job. Then imagine turning and looking back toward now, and ask your unconscious mind to align all the events from now to then. Cross your hands in the center of your chest, and take a deep breath of release as you open your eyes.

Do this visualization once a day, preferably just before you go to sleep, so that your unconscious mind is programmed for high-energy results. The most important thing to remember with visualization is that you must dissociate yourself at the end and imagine yourself as your own observer—so that the unconscious mind knows that it has not happened yet. Manipulation, by the way, does not work with this exercise, so if it is not for your highest good, it may not happen. For example, if you want to marry Tony or Jane and Tony or Jane is not interested, visualizing a marriage with him or her may not work (we all have free choice).

So, use your date as your key point. If Tony or Jane has not shown any interest by the date you envisioned, change the scenario to "Congratulations! You have just become engaged to the perfect man (or woman) for you!" Put in a new date. By opening up to endless possibilities, you often actualize much better than you ever dreamed.

Words for an Infinity of Possibilities

Begin by sitting down and doing Magic of the Mind Three. At the end, take the breath and release it as you direct your unconscious mind:

Release all nonsupportive beliefs and limiting decisions about being 100 percent successful and happy, while preserving all of the positive lessons. Yes! Yes! Yes!

Then follow the same process exactly as before.

Dale, a telemarketer, was really excited to take my seven-day training to change her career direction. She didn't have the money in advance to pay for the course, so I suggested postdated checks. She leapt at the chance.

Two weeks before the course started, Dale paid for the entire training in a lump sum payment when a yearly disbursement arrived unexpectedly from her financial planner. In her phone message she simply said: "Ta da! Look in your mailbox!"

She told me later, "Seven days of changing my language and thinking in a really fun way made me realize that I only have to ask clearly with intent for my wants to be met."

However, even I was astounded when the normally cautious Dale turned up on the first day with a new car, because otherwise it would have meant her traveling three hours each way, every day, to attend the training! She had simply decided to have faith just as I'd told her. I didn't realize that I was so persuasive. So before she even began the training, everything started falling into place and coming together for her.

I love this high-energy word magic! Changing people's lives for the better has to be the best job in the world.

Vision Board

The Vision Board or Wheel of Fortune is a very powerful means of creating something wonderful—and it works! Many thanks to my lovely friend Colette Baron-Reid (intuitive, recording artist, and bestselling author) for this one.

On a piece of cardboard or poster board, section off parts, like in a pie chart, and give each part a focus: family, health, your love life, travel and leisure, and of course career or money or home. Draw a very clear boundary all along the edges of the board. This detail is very important: it acts as a "body" or vessel, giving symbolic form to its contents. In each of these, paste pictures, drawings, or actual photographs (perhaps out of magazines)—things that you feel symbolize the optimum conditions and results for that category. Write a date underneath each photo or drawing that is sometime in the next twelve months.

Add affirmations, detailed statements of what you want achieved, and state them in the NOW, as if they have already happened. Put the board on a door or wall where you will see it every day. Read it on a daily basis to help stimulate those thought magnets, and keep them consistent. *You will get results!*

Rich and Loving It

When do you begin? NOW! NOW! and NOW! again. The right time is always now. This is the most powerful minute of your life, as you have the opportunity right now to make your future happen.

Money is simply an exchange of energy; the more energy you spend to make it happen, the more success (and money) you receive back. Use your own natural talents, along with feel-good language, thoughts, and actions, to bring you the success that is rightfully yours. Just follow these easy keys for financial happiness:

1. **Love yourself.** Walk tall, talk and act like a Prince or Princess. Look at yourself in the mirror every day and say: "Gorgeous!" The true foundation of money and prosperity is self-worth. Yes, I know that there are rich people who don't like themselves. However, you want to be rich *and* happy don't you?

2. **Pay attention to your thoughts and commit to clear thinking, clear intent, and clear action.** Choose to switch your thinking and speaking to become a success and power magnet.

3. **Play to win/win.** Reach for the stars. Make sure that everyone and everything benefits by your actions.

4. **Demand positive attention.** We all love and long for attention, so say daily: *It's time now for me to get attention in healthy, positive ways that constantly bring me passion, power, and fulfillment.*

5. **Read motivational books, or listen to success tapes** (go to my website, *www.YvonneOswald.com*, for some great CDs on prosperity, self-worth, and abundance).

6. **Be happy when others make it**, because when you're successful others can be happy for you, too.

7. **Surround yourself with high-energy, powerful people.** Join a golf/tennis/fitness club where successful people go.

8. **Find simple solutions.** Write down situations and then write down possible solutions or ways to make them easier. Make a decision to do one of them, and just do it! If no solutions are forthcoming, make a decision to think about it later, and let it go for now. Trust your unconscious mind to come up with a new solution within twenty-four hours.

9. **Ask for help.** It gives someone an opportunity to feel great. Your gift to them is to allow them to give you a gift.

10. **Have fun making money.** Go wild every now and again by splurging to give you the feeling of abundance. Open a special bottle for an un-celebration (for no other reason than the fact that you can).

11. **Weed out your low-energy qualities and patterns** as though weeding a garden. As you notice any less than admirable traits, switch them.

12. **Spend time every day being thankful** for what you have, and praise yourself for who you are and what you're achieving. Only you can make yourself happy.

Create Your Whole New World

Reconnect now with all the abundance of high-energy emotions: excitement, love, passion, joy, happiness, compassion for yourself and others. Successful people make lots of decisions and make them quickly. You take the feedback from whatever emerges from your decisions and decide what else you need to learn to make success happen. You believe wholeheartedly in what you are doing. You live your life with passion and power. To be truly successful, the results you produce (be they financial, emotional, physical, or mental) benefit not only yourself, but others around you (a win/win situation), including the planet.

You are accountable. You assume that even if something is not your "fault," you can still do something to rectify and change it, becoming totally empowered. Fear and doubt are emotions of the middle brain. These emotions will inhibit success, because it is in the higher mind—the cerebral cortex, the mind of the imagination—where success originates.

You can believe in "fate" or "bad luck," or you can decide now that even if fate happens, you still have choices. You are either in harmony with God or the universe, or you are not. For one month (or your whole life) think of life's events as a mirror. If you meet someone who is angry, ask yourself about what or with whom *you yourself* are angry. If you meet a successful, happy person, congratulate yourself. If things are not going right, ask yourself, "What lesson is this teaching me, or what can I take from this? What else do I need to know? *And what can I do about it right now?*"

This is the most important part because being accountable means taking action *every* time so that you are always moving forward toward your success. Excitement and curiosity are qualities that I hope you will keep throughout your whole life. Give everything in your life 100 percent and enjoy using these wonderful tools that bring you satisfaction and joy. Life is a dance.

As *Star Trek*'s Captain Jean-Luc Picard of the USS *Enterprise* says, *"Make it so!"*

Recap

1. Model yourself on someone you admire, or look up to, who is successful. (Remember the story of Good King Wenceslas? The page trod in the king's footsteps to walk more easily through the snow.) It's easier to copy a model than to create a whole new one. Stay true to your values.
2. Be passionate. Love *everything* you're doing all the time, and when you do not love it, take the lesson and learn from it.
3. Dream big. Look out for new opportunities every day. Take action to make things happen.
4. Be specific and realistic. Take chances, and correct as you go along.
5. Be generous and kind to yourself every day. Be adventurous as you try on all the other emotions and states: joy, happiness, love, passion, power, kindness, fun, and enjoyment.

6. Follow the process:
- *Motivation*—Why do I want it?
- *Intention*—What's the true objective?
- *Action*—How can I get it? What's the very first step?
- *Expectation*—What emotion makes me know I really want it?
- *Flexibility*—Plan for the best and change as I go.
- *Gratitude*—I'm thankful for every change, good or not good.

7. Live the best life you can. Give 100 percent to play, work, rest, exercise, healthy eating, communicating, and fun!

Each morning as you awake you have a choice. You can choose to let the day just happen, or you can choose to direct and plan every new day to create a masterpiece.

Chapter Four Action Plan

Keys to Success and Happiness

1. Stay motivated.

Spend the first half hour after you wake up anchoring a high-energy state. Remember all the most wonderful times of your life. Get up fifteen minutes earlier to exercise, meditate, do self-hypnosis, or listen to motivational CDs.

2. Prioritize. Be self-motivated.

If your daily list is long, do the three priority goals. Observe any distraction techniques in the form of "busy" jobs that you find yourself doing, or when you get involved in other people's dramas. Thank your unconscious mind for making you aware, and then get back to the plan!

3. Focus on what you want and need.

Write down your three simple daily goals to make them real. Read them aloud to breathe life into them. Do more than three, and you're in bonus points. Congratulations!

4. **Create new opportunities.**

   Call people. Sign up for courses, especially something you would not usually study—belly dancing, rock climbing—and get out of the box! Join the Chamber of Commerce and groups of people working *toward* something. Be creative. Make something. Decorate your house or have a makeover.

5. **Take time off.**

   Write "ME TIME" in your calendar and take at least half an hour for yourself. Stretch and breathe for two minutes. Treat yourself to a special coffee or tea. Listen to music. Dance or have fun for five minutes. Take a hot bath or shower.

6. **Be productive.**

   Make one call you need to make. Pay one bill you need to pay. Do ten minutes of exercise. Eat nine foods of different colors (as little brown food as possible). Thank someone. Praise someone. Remember that your unconscious mind thinks you're talking about yourself.

7. **Be grateful for three or more things today.**

   Gratitude is an expansive feeling that opens up the window to joy and manifestation. Be thankful for the sunshine, the birds singing, your home, your own skills, and special people in your life. Ask yourself, "What am I thankful for right now?" on the hour every hour. If the answer comes back "Nothing," then thank yourself for the information, and make a decision to go and find something to be thankful for.

8. **Believe.**

   What you believe and perceive becomes your reality that you then believe and perceive! It's time to make a decision to believe in what's working, and if anything isn't working, realize that there's something that may need changing.

9. **Choose today.**

   Focus now on life-affirming language, high-energy attitude, and success-oriented actions. Consciously use high-energy words such as success, happiness, joy, optimism, laugh, prosperity, and health in your daily conversations.

10. **Reward yourself and have fun.**

 Enjoy life. Before you go to sleep, ask yourself, "What did I do well today? What did I not do well? Why did I choose to create that? What reward did I give myself today? What can I do tomorrow that will make me happier?" Say to yourself, "I'm so looking forward to a great day tomorrow! I love life."

11. **Enjoy fortune cookies without the calories!**

 Write out affirmations on slips of paper, fold them twice, and then place them in a basket or bowl. Choose one each morning, read it aloud, and repeat it seven times that day. You can also paste these individual affirmations near a light switch, on a mirror, or anywhere else you see or touch on a regular basis. Expect great results.

12. **Live joyfully.**

 Dwell in a constant state of exuberance—of wonderful things happening. Have fun.

5

The Power of
Letting Go

*Your emotions are like an orchestra, with your
unconscious mind as the conductor, fear as the cymbal,
and anger as the big bass drum.*

The orchestra of your feelings can be sweet and harmonious or produce a confused sound that feels like chaos. It only takes one out-of-tune instrument to cause an interruption to the music's flow. When you're in tune with yourself and your destiny, your inner orchestra is synchronized, forming a dynamic coherence of high-energy emotions that produce endorphins in your biophysical body, making you feel wonderful and allowing your imagination to soar.

You set up an attraction pattern with your thoughts and words—a magnetic force field of energies searching for other, similar energies. You are naturally a seeker. Your deepest neural networks are programmed to complete patterns. What will you be able to achieve when you have at your fingertips the vast resources of the quantum universe by simply sending out a word or thought? Anything? Everything!

Words Trigger Emotions

All of your emotional responses are valuable, including those low-energy ones you'd rather do without, such as anger, sadness, fear, guilt, and anxiety. Each is designed to ensure survival, both individually and collectively as a species. Emotions are simply information—labels that we give to feelings produced by the unconscious mind in response to a word, thought, or event. Every word you speak or think has at least three chains of meanings associated with it, rather like strings of Christmas tree lights: 1) a chain that represents your own individual feelings, based on your memory of events; 2) a chain from your genetically inherited feelings; and 3) a chain based on the collective unconscious, or group memory.

The word "mother" has a different chain of meaning for you than me, as do "father," "sister," and "grandmother." The more the intensity of emotion associated with a word, the more it will affect your decision-making strategies. The word "chair," for instance, has a much shorter chain of meaning for most people and will not usually trigger deep feelings. Emotions are the daily system your unconscious mind uses as a signal that you're in or out of tune. Your dreams are one of the ways the unconscious attempts to communicate this balance and sort out the feelings.

As much as we'd like to believe that we use logic to make decisions, every decision we make is based on a need to produce a satisfactory result—in other words, to make us feel better. Emotions can bypass the filter of your conscious mind because they are instinctive. They underlie everything you do. They are your mind messengers, your litmus paper of life. Simply watch a baby to discover how fast emotions can come and go.

If your thoughts are interrupted by a negative thought or a nonsupportive belief, the clear signal wavers and inconsistent results are generated. When something is *not* running smoothly, no matter how much you think you can control it consciously, your inner mind will signal you in a flash by manifesting what it believes to be the right emotion for the circumstance or event.

The technology behind lie detectors is based on this instant mind/body connection.

Strong or intense feelings also interfere with the transmission of the correct communication signal. According to how the information was stored and what was distorted, deleted, or generalized, the word or thought will already have emotions attached to it, and retrieval may produce some interesting results. We've all had an experience, perhaps at a wedding or a funeral, where an unreasonable amount of emotion surfaced at something someone said quite innocently.

Another time that the unconscious mind searches out and produces an inappropriate response is if your conscious mind filters are too strong. The reason for this may be that you have made a nonsupportive decision in the past, or that you've instructed the unconscious on some level that you have been compromised or that survival depends on your being right. That doesn't necessarily mean that you *are* right, just that you believe that you are!

So, how do you use this knowledge to your benefit? Remember that in chapter two we talked about the hidden variable of the quantum field potential, that, when activated, brings you amazing future possibilities? In the realm of emotions, it's the wild card of *dynamic excitability*. By getting excited you increase and speed up your chances of success. Overstimulation is not the same as excitement, by the way. Exciting emotions include enthusiasm and passion, but also include anger and fear; that's why you seem to attract a lot more negative events when you are feeling really down. In fact, you also attract more positive events when you feel up, but you don't notice them as much because you just feel so great.

There are four kinds of emotions:

1. *Positive revitalizing emotions* such as excitement, passion, ardor, desire, elation, ecstasy, inspiration, joy, and love, which always take you to a place of optimism and motivate you to progress forward to take action
2. *Negative stimulating emotions* such as anger, rage, and fear, which have a temporary boosting effect, but produce

extremely inconsistent results: sometimes propelling you forward, but just as often backward or even downward

3. *Negative devitalizing emotions* such as envy, despair, sadness, depression, grief, remorse, shame, sorrow, and guilt, which slow down or bring to a halt any action, progress, or results

4. *Neutralizing emotions* such as anxiety, regret, unease, and indecision, which serve to produce inertia and immobilization of action

Any low-energy word, thought, emotion, or belief interferes with and interrupts your access to love, joy, and abundance (those little clouds hiding the sunshine again). Success then becomes unpredictable. What also acts as an interruption to happiness is the belief that fear, anger, guilt, self-doubt, and old limiting decisions are real. These emotions of the middle brain are a linear reality—a delusion. They are there simply to let you know that new action is needed.

When you open up to the idea that these old low-energy emotions do not really exist, that they are simply names you give to feelings to describe an absence of love and joy, you move toward life-enhancing awareness and pure consciousness. You go from polarity to oneness. You allow yourself to regain power, passion, confidence, and self-worth. You have more clarity, lucidity, and understanding as you move toward your ultimate potential.

So how do you change the set-point of your happiness thermostat to high? You focus on clearing negative emotions as they come up on a daily basis, while examining any nonsupportive beliefs, and then concentrate on increasing your strengths. Get enthusiastic, find something beautiful to appreciate, renew your sense of curiosity and love of learning, and find fun and humor in every event.

Before you can establish these great habits, you first need to clear out the less supportive ones to bring you to an optimum level of health. Then you can build vital, additional behaviors to support the new states.

Your Health Is Truly Your Wealth

Remembering that the prime directive of your unconscious mind is to keep you healthy and alive, let's start making major changes by reviewing your health. When people talk about their health, they're usually referring to their physical bodies. We actually have four bodies to keep healthy: spiritual, mental, emotional, and physical.

A blockage or imbalance in one or more of the four bodies causes discomfort, eventually lowering the immune system. I'm going to show you how to clear your mental and emotional body by changing your thoughts and language patterns, and finally, how to address and clear the physical body. Then we can move on to fill the newly opened space with great new strategies to bring you success in every area of your life.

Currently there are well over a billion Internet sites devoted to health. The word "health" is derived from the Anglo-Saxon word "hale" (as in "hale and hearty") meaning whole, complete. "Holy" has the same origin. That being so, there must be a connection between being healthy and being connected to the source of all power and light: oneness, spirit, or God. You are not alone. Your unconscious mind is standing with you, ready to be your guardian angel or your own personal genie.

Be Careful: Your Mind Is Listening

Every one of the trillions of cells that make up your body remembers and stores the memory of every event, feeling, or thought you've ever experienced. If you have ever watched a child being admonished, you will notice that the child's body becomes as small as possible in defense. The child holds his or her breath and the fear of the moment is then stored somewhere in the body, providing a temporary blockage in the natural energy flow.

Repeated verbal or physical punishment has a more lasting effect. Repression and suppression lead to aggression. Your unconscious mind will do everything it can to protect you from a perceived threat, so if there's been repeated negative impact from someone (particularly a parent or caregiver), the subsequent emotional reaction may be extreme as your unconscious mind tries to get your attention. Depending on a person's coping strategies, he or she may hurt others, hurt themselves, or simply not be able to relate to others and withdraw. If the person is not able to resolve the situation and let it go, constant stress or anxiety is the result.

According to the Public Health Service, about 50 percent of mental health issues reported in the United States (apart from substance misuse) are accounted for by anxiety disorders. The goal of any kind of therapy is to release these old patterns or blockages (which can be physical, emotional, mental, or spiritual). You are the engineer of your health, just as you are the engineer of your own happiness, success, and well-being.

Both the Chinese *chi* energy system and the Japanese *ki* system explain that blockages in your electrical messaging system, through negative thinking, unhealthy eating, or emotional repression, eventually manifest physically in the form of disease. Lack and limitation are defined by how many nonsupportive beliefs (not good enough, not clever enough) and low-energy emotions (anger, sadness, guilt, shame, fear, and anxiety) are stored in the unconscious mind. In order to balance the energy and recover, we need to review our thinking patterns, core beliefs, eating, and exercise.

So for all of you who've been sitting on the edge of your seats, waiting for the biggest, fastest, and best Magic of the Mind trick, this is it: Magic of the Mind Six is an amazing way to clear anxiety, negative emotions, and nonsupportive beliefs ... even old, long-standing ones. You can do this exercise as many times as you want to every day to immediately clear any low-energy emotion or state. The more often you do it, the quicker your unconscious mind will learn to let go in the future, without any conscious instruction from you. To begin, we have some preparation so that you know how to do each of the stages separately.

Magic of the Mind Six

Preparation:
Know how to go into the alpha state, as in Magic of the Mind Three, and know how to anchor.

Review of Magic of the Mind Three

As you sit comfortably with your back straight, face forward with your chin slightly up, and raise your eyes to ceiling level. Find a place where the ceiling meets the wall and simply stare at that spot. Now become aware of what's to your right and what's to your left, while keeping your eyes and head in the same place; be aware of what's in your peripheral vision. Notice the nice, relaxed feeling you get when you do this. You will practice this in step three below.

Anchoring

Take your left hand and rest it in a loose fist on your left thigh (if you're left-handed, use your right hand on your right thigh if you wish). Then simply place the tip of the index finger of your right hand on top of the knuckle of your left index finger (where the finger meets the hand). This is called an "anchor," and anchors the new state into your body.

Now, are you ready to proceed with Magic of the Mind Six?

1. Sit with your back straight, left hand in a loose fist on your left knee, and right hand relaxed on your right knee.
2. Think of the emotion, belief, or memory you most want to clear. Put your head down; close your eyes if you like, to access it fully.
3. When you can *really* feel the negative emotion, put your head up and open your eyes. Look up and go into the alpha state of Magic of the Mind Three.

4. Now do the anchoring. Take the tip of your right index finger, put it on top of the first knuckle of your left hand, and hold it there.
5. Still holding the anchor and with your eyes still open, take a deep breath and breathe out powerfully as you say aloud to your unconscious mind: "*Release the root cause of the* _____ *(name the negative emotion or nonsupportive decision) plus all other negative emotions and negative beliefs around this whole area, while preserving all the positive lessons for my health and benefit.*"
6. Remove the anchor by separating your hands.
7. Put your head down again and access the negative state. You won't find the feelings as easily this time.
8. Repeat steps 1 through 5.
9. Repeat steps 6 and 7. Try in vain to find the negative emotion or state. It's gone.

Access (or attempt to access) the negative state three times to ensure that it's completely gone. Amazing, isn't it? I love to do this Magic of the Mind with clients to show them how easy it is to clear old low-energy feelings. We chose the least good moment of their lives to have really great proof that it works. Your unconscious mind is very happy to let go because it's healthy to clear out low-energy emotions. Ideally let go of the emotions in this order: anger, then sadness, then guilt, then fear.

The more you do this, the more you'll start to feel in control of your emotional state. Then, if you're ever feeling less than good, simply by putting your finger on the knuckle again, you'll go into that wonderful alpha state. I spent an hour at the dentist's with my finger on top of my knuckle, and I felt great the entire time.

I've found the best and easiest way to clear and release deep-seated negative emotions permanently is with Memory Continuum Therapy, my own adaptation and extension of Time Line Therapy™. This method takes you back to before the original event (and before the gestalt, or sequence of events, that followed) to release low-energy emotions, while preserving all the positive learnings. By finding the root cause of the emotion or belief, clients transform their perspective of life in just one breakthrough session. The unconscious mind is very happy to let go of negative behaviors or feelings once it's convinced that you understand what it was trying to tell you.

Control or Control Issues?

By experiencing events with objectivity, you regain control of your life. Being in control means that you can make better choices and decisions. Are you in control of your life in every area? Do you feel that you are aware of and using all of your potential? If not, you may find that some low-energy emotions and events begin to arrive in your life as your unconscious mind tries to draw your attention to the fact that something is not balanced. At this point, being in control may be replaced by control issues: the inappropriate need to control people or events outside of yourself due to the absence of real control. Life management may then be replaced with a constant need for perfection as you try to keep ahead of the surfacing feelings of discomfort.

The names we've given to the main feelings of discomfort are anger, sadness/depression, fear, and guilt. Let's go ahead and find more ways to clear these low-energy feelings, one by one, to enable you to regain your vitality and empower you to create your new, fabulous life.

How do you release negative emotions if they do come up? One of the quickest ways if you haven't got a therapist within reach is to do physical exercise of any kind. The workout preferably needs to make you breathe heavily, so sex is as good an exercise as running! Physical exercise allows you to take the energy and channel it into something productive. It also clears toxins and negative emotions as a by-product. Then do Magic of the Mind Six to feel better instantly.

Another way is to increase and free the energy attached to the emotion by using a sounding technique. All energy produces resonance, which produces sound. The reason that this exercise works was proven in a Japanese university. They developed a method for erasing sound by using the sound of an opposing frequency. Sounds of opposite frequency cannot resonate. In fact, by creating the exact opposite noise, researchers can eliminate the original sound. Ideally, this exercise is done in a place away from other people, as it can be very loud.

Magic of the Mind Seven

Whenever you are in the car, or in the bath or shower, choose a low-energy word that resonates with you at the time (anger, fear, guilt, shame, or sadness) or choose a high-energy word (love, peace, calm, joy, happy, passion, or power). Take your attention to—or just think about—your power center, which is three finger widths below your belly button. Take a deep breath, and call or sing the word as loud and as long as you can. It does not matter how naughty or how spiritual the word is; simply think of a word without judgment! The emphasis is on the vowel sound, so the word "fear," being a vowel digraph, would sound like: "Feeeee ... eeeee ... aaaaaaaaaarrrr!"

Continue the vowel sound for at least a minute, until you can feel the muscles in your belly go tight and your face is red! The sound "eeeee," by the way, opens the heart center, and "aaaaaah" opens the third eye energy center, which increases intuition and manifestation. A great way to do this is to face a wall or door close up and pretend that you can blow a hole in it with your voice.

You can sound someone's name or call out "Meeeeeeeeeeeee!" as loud as you like. Or call out "Freeeeeeeeeeeeeeeeeeeeeeeeeee!" The longer and more intense the vowel sound is, the quicker you'll feel reenergized and great! You can sing the sound more softly if, for instance, you are living in an apartment and noise is not encouraged; however, the vowel sound then needs to be held for longer.

By the time you get to the quiet space at the end of the noise you've made, you've eliminated any unwanted emotion by changing the frequency of the sound attached to it and clearing the way for a pleasant emotion to take its place. I've had some funny looks from people when I've done this at a traffic light, so find a place where you can make noise alone!

An interesting variation of this exercise is to choose a part of your body that doesn't feel great and imagine, or pretend, to know what word would be there if you have to choose a word or feeling. Sound that word, and then ask yourself what word is underneath it. Keep going until you recover a high-energy word like "love" or "safe." Sound that word, and you'll feel wonderful. This is also a great method for releasing physical pain from the body.

Clear the Anger

Anger is a wonderful emotional energy that can be used to stimulate action. Many great changes in society have been made by someone getting angry enough to make a difference. In its less useful form, anger is an emotion that is often due to unrealistic and unfulfilled entitlement or expectations. It's a need for control or power. The energy becomes inappropriate when it is internalized without being released productively or constructively. The opposite, high-energy emotion to anger is passion, which is a great way to channel anger if it *does* come up to the surface.

Anger is mainly found where boundaries have been crossed (imaginary or otherwise), or when your values have been compromised, such as if you perceive an injustice. It can also be found when childhood situations are triggered by current events, as your unconscious mind attempts to bring to the surface any unresolved issues in order to clear away old emotional baggage.

There are two types of anger that we need to address. The first is situational, or anger due to outside circumstances, such as when someone steps on your toe or you find that the person you came to visit isn't in. This is called externalized anger. Magic of the Mind Six is great for this.

The other type is deeper: internalized anger. It's the slow burn that is felt just under the surface of awareness, which may pop up at any time, and is usually related to issues originating in childhood (or before). If Magic of the Mind Six, physical exercise, and Magic of the Mind Seven don't clear it, then this anger is something that needs to be addressed by a professional. Again, Memory Continuum Therapy and hypnotherapy are the fastest tools available for this anger release.

There are over two hundred known uses for hypnosis, by the way. All hypnosis is self-hypnosis, so you are in total control when you are doing it. It was accepted as a natural wellness tool in 1956 by the Catholic Church, and by the American Medical Association in 1958. A survey of psychotherapy literature by Alfred A. Barrios, PhD, published in *American Health* magazine revealed the following recovery rates:

- Psychoanalysis: 38 percent recovery after six hundred sessions
- Behavior therapy: 72 percent recovery after twenty-two sessions
- Hypnotherapy: 93 percent recovery after six sessions

Obviously, the real key is to prevent anger by staying relaxed and aware of any situation that would induce a feeling of lack of control or intrusion into your space. Also, remember to clear the word "anger" from your language patterns. Switch to "strong emotion." Some other solutions for clearing anger:

- Fresh fruits and vegetables
- Cleansing: physical toxins can often manifest as negative emotions
- Exercise: aerobic or alpha-stimulating, such as yoga or lane swimming
- Singing
- Deep breathing
- High-energy thinking and speaking
- Meditation
- Sleep

For Deeper Anger Release

Find a trusted therapist. Memory Continuum Therapy or hypnosis is ideal for internalized anger and for finding the root cause. Laughter is also a great way to clear anger. You can't be angry and laugh at the same time.

When anger is released, sadness often surfaces.

Sadness Release

Crying is a great way to release sadness. Find all the sad CDs or cassettes you can, or get ready to replay all the sad scenes from a movie that you know will help you to cry, and get them set up for two hours. At nine o'clock *exactly*, press the play button and really, really feel sorry for yourself. Then concentrate on finding understanding and compassion for yourself. You have innate integrity and an ability to discover your own unique truth about your life. Allow yourself the grace of grieving, as you would allow for someone else. By validating unhappiness and intensifying it, you let it go. I've never managed to cry for the whole two hours when I do this. I run out of things to think about long before eleven o'clock, and I reward myself with a good book, music, or a special treat. The time limit is the most important element in this exercise because giving yourself a fixed time sets a boundary and gives permission to the unconscious mind for quick release of the emotions. Also, by getting the conscious mind involved and engaged again you gain objectivity, which will begin to loosen the old emotions.

Your physical body will give you a big clue if emotions are imbalanced for any length of time. Your dis-ease will result in just that . . . disease. One of the most common emotional dis-eases of this century has been depression.

Depression

Depression is an external trigger related to a sense of loss. It's about feeling that you do not have the power to express yourself, or have not given yourself permission to do so. It's usually caused by unresolved anger. It's devitalizing. It has come to mean disappointment, as in "I'm depressed that I didn't get what I wanted for my birthday." It's a natural phenomenon that happens when someone is conscious of feeling overwhelmed. As a temporary external condition it can be useful; it allows a person to take time off from feelings to bring his or her emotions back into balance. It makes the person feel that they need to take time out to do ... nothing. A quick solution for feeling down is to just do exactly that: watch a DVD or read a book. Pray. Give your spirit a rest.

Someone who is deeply depressed for any length of time needs a support system from an external source such as friends or a therapist, who will work with him or her to help to become more objective. A good way to distract the person from the depression is by interrupting the pattern, perhaps in the form of a night out, or bringing fresh information in by learning something new. Memory Continuum and/or hypnosis are again my therapies of choice for finding root causes for low emotions.

Fear

Fear is simply the absence of trust. Are you happy, healthy, loved, prosperous, adventurous, confident, and comfortable in your environment and home? If not, do you trust that you are heading in that direction? Or are you living in fear? Fear keeps people from having all of the wonderful moments in life.

The inappropriate need to be in control is either fear-based or anger-based. If anger is a feeling of not being in control, fear is a feeling that you are being controlled by someone or something outside yourself, which is not actually possible! There are currently tens of millions of websites on the Internet devoted to fears and phobias. The only thing to *really* be afraid of is standing still for too long, or fear itself.

Fear is a primary survival response, which was very useful in the past, when we had to take action by fighting or fleeing from predators since fear increases alertness. The hormones produced by a fear response are mainly adrenaline and cortisol, which produce physical sensations of dry mouth, increased heart and respiration rate, insomnia, increased blood pressure, and a sensation of fluttering in the stomach area. When the fear is over, a sense of release or euphoria is experienced. These days, we even induce fear for fun just to get the high that results from a fear response. It's great in small doses; just go on a roller coaster ride, bungee jump, or go whitewater rafting. Your alertness is increased and you feel more alive.

The modern-day fears of not having enough, being enough, or doing enough are more abstract and yet bring the same physiological response, without the subsequent release. Action is needed, just as it was needed in the past, to bring fulfillment and meaning to your life.

Ask yourself this: "What am I afraid of most: not being enough, not doing enough, or not having enough?" Then ask, "What is it that I am not being, am not doing, or don't have?" It's useful to write down the answer so that you can more easily find a solution and take action.

Fear of failure is not the only fear people have. People can be just as afraid of success due to old ideas or nonsupportive beliefs about it. Remember that love, money, health, comfort, and purpose are your reward and your right.

Fear and judgment create separation. Clearing fear opens up enormous inner resources and psychological strength. When abundance and trust are present in every area of your life, fear is absent. It's unusual to wake up in the morning and feel concerned about whether there is enough air for you to breathe all day. You just take it for granted. There is enough air for us all—and more. So how do you feel about having an abundance of love, money, and health?

Are you really ready for it all?

It's Time to Make Changes

Find the courage inside you to change. Do *anything* different— especially things that are "not you." If being "you" hasn't made you happy so far, having a go at new things must be worth something! Sitting on the fence is not pleasant for very long; your unconscious mind will find a way to change you sooner or later.

The universe is an ever-unfolding flower that changes nanosecond by nanosecond. Make those changes. Change what you normally have for breakfast. Change your routine. Decide to change your job and your home, and improve your relationships. You don't feel comfortable changing one of these? Then change everything else *except* the thing you most need to change and then that last one will change automatically! The key to clearing fear is decision-making and forward-moving action.

Clear the Fear

Before we look at fear release, you might want to find your own safe place to have as a retreat if at any time you feel less than comfortable. Your unconscious mind knows what it needs to do in order to let go of any stored, low-energy emotions and will not allow you to experience something you are not ready to process. However, it is sometimes good to have your "safe spot" as a backup.

Imagine your dream relaxation holiday. It might be a beach, a forest glade, a mountain, a wood with a stream running through it, or a temple. Anywhere that you would feel totally safe is fine. Close your eyes and for two minutes imagine as vividly as you can that you are in your safe spot. Can you feel the water? Smell the air? Feel the sun on your face or the breeze in your hair? What can you hear? What taste is in your mouth? Paint your safe place as colorfully as you can.

Now, imagine the sun pouring from the sky into the top of your head, and stretch lazily. If you wish, you can erect a fence or a forest around your safe place.

Transform the Fear: An Exercise

Much of our fear is inherited, picked up from our parents' fears during the imprinting phase, the first seven years of childhood. So, it's important that we recognize and release not only what we think of as our own fears, but also the fears we took on without realizing. Sit comfortably for this exercise. Play some quiet music, or stay in silence. Close your eyes and relax.

Imagine that you are in a private room. There is a door to your right and a window to your left. Outside is a beautiful day. The sun is shining brightly and you can see through the window into a park or garden. Observe the door opening. Imagine your mother's biggest fear coming in through the door. What would it look like if you can imagine it as a small person with a face, two arms, and two legs? Observe this person moving to the side of your bed and say "hello" to them. How do you feel about this person? What is his or her name? Make up the first name that comes into your head. Can you find it in yourself to feel sorry for the person, knowing the kind of life he or she has had? What can you do to the fear to make this person beautiful? Ask what he or she needs from you to help. Use your imagination to do anything you can do to make the person friendly or comfortable.

Some suggestions:

1. Take him or her into the sunlight.
2. Make the person smaller so that you can cuddle and comfort him or her to make them feel better.
3. Get a nurse, an angel, or a visitor to come in to help you.
4. Give him or her a gift.
5. Help the person step out of his or her "skin" to find out if there's someone nice underneath.
6. Touch him or her softly and say that you care for them.
7. Use a magic wand to transform the fear into something beautiful.

After the person feels better, offer freedom through an open door or window (watch him or her disappear, change into a butterfly, or walk out).

Repeat the exercise for your father's fear, and then repeat it again for your own fear. Remember to retreat to your "safe place" if you need to, for just a second or two, and then go back to the exercise.

Magic of the Mind Eight will show you how to create a feeling of safety when you need it.

Magic of the Mind Eight

An Exercise to Feel Safe:

This exercise can be done anywhere. The key to its success is to change your physiology. Make sure that your back is straight, your head is erect, and your chin is tilted slightly upward.

Imagine above you the most beautiful sun—a disc of yellow energy. Breathe in the sun to the count of seven. Hold the energy in the center of your chest to the count of seven, and then release it slowly to the count of eleven. As you release, imagine yourself surrounded by a beautiful protective bubble of radiant energy. You might want to pray or feel thankful to raise your vibration higher.

Breathe the light in again and imagine yourself in the most beautiful place you can think of. Remember a time when you felt really safe. It could be a childhood memory, a new love, or a recent promotion. Find every instance of happiness and safety in your memory bank, and when you find one that makes you feel good, stay with it. Remember how wonderful that moment felt.

Where are you holding that memory in your physical body? If you don't know, where in your body would it be if you had to choose a place? Continue the breathing until your heartbeat and breathing rate slow down.

Anxiety

Anxiety is a state of uncertainty or uneasiness about a future-based event. It is different from fear, inasmuch as fear is an instinctive neurological response to a current event or to the memory of a past event. Anxiety is not, strictly speaking, an emotion because it is a response to something that hasn't happened yet. However, it's very real for those who experience it, and is both debilitating and neutralizing in its effect.

If you are facing a dog just about to attack, your response is not anxiety, it's fear, because the fight-or-flight survival response kicks in. If you are concerned about dogs biting you when there's no good reason that they would, that's anxiety. The label we give to an unreasonably extreme recurring reaction like this is "phobia."

The first thing to do to clear anxiety is to simply imagine the best-case scenario. What is the last thing that would have to happen to convince you that you can feel great about the situation? If it's anxiety about a job interview, would it be the person interviewing you and shaking your hand in congratulations? If it's a date, would it be the person saying what a wonderful night he or she had and asking to see you again? If it's public speaking, would it be the crowd shouting and cheering and giving you a standing ovation?

Then close your eyes and imagine floating above your body to just after the *successful* completion of the event. Imagine floating down into your body, and really feel the wonderful experience of success. Brighten the colors; smell and taste and hear everything; think about how you feel. Is the anxiety gone now? If necessary, do Magic of the Mind Six. Ask your unconscious mind to preserve the positive lessons while releasing the negative emotions, and then get back to your wonderful life.

Guilt and Shame

Guilt is one of the most unpleasant emotions to carry around. It comes from the Anglo-Saxon word "gylt," meaning sin or crime. It's really nature's way of giving us a conscience so that we can support the group. Guilt is the word we use for the low-energy emotion that people feel when they've disappointed others. Shame is the feeling that comes when they are disappointed with themselves. Guilt, shame, and resentment are the emotions that are most draining of one's energy and resources. They are devitalizing in the extreme. Low-energy thoughts and a lowered immune system may result from harboring any of these low-frequency feelings for any length of time (longer than two minutes!).

One of the most interesting cases of inappropriate guilt was revealed in a therapy session I facilitated with a lady in her thirties. When I asked Sylvia why she had come, she told me that she had a very happy marriage, great children, a wonderful house, an amazing job, and superb health. I couldn't imagine why that would have led her to me. It turned out that the reason she wasn't enjoying her life was because she felt constant guilt about the fact that others didn't have all that she had. When she realized that as a child her mother had instilled in her the belief that she didn't deserve to have much, we released the old negative emotions and nonsupportive decisions and she left, floating on air—off to enjoy her life fully.

Resentment

Holding a grievance or grudge separates people from themselves and separates them from truth and joy. This separation leads to outward projection, resulting in imbalance. In reality, not forgiving others means that self-forgiveness and self-acceptance are absent.

Research from the Johns Hopkins University indicates that long-term and unresolved resentment is a possible way to get cancer, because when people see themselves as victims, the guilt that is projected onto the perpetrator has to return as punishment— particularly guilt held at an unconscious level.

Any unresolved emotional issue will eventually show up in the physical body. Your body has no choice but to express whatever emotions you suppress. Pain is the ultimate message from your unconscious mind to let you know that you're not listening yet! I treat all physical illness as a limiting belief that came from a limiting decision.

Harboring a grudge is also extremely devitalizing. It's not always easy to address people from your past to balance out the issue. And telling someone to just get over it is not very effective. So how can you let go? The Hawaiian people have a wonderful exercise that they do for release and forgiveness. They call it *Ho'oponopono*. In the appendix is my adaptation of this forgiveness and release process, a script that you can record in your own voice and listen to every day until you feel revitalized. You'll be amazed at the results. A CD of this script (with original music) is available at *www.YvonneOswald.com*.

As you learn to accept others and appreciate them for their courage, you may recognize that people are not their behaviors. Truly look to find the five-year-old in everyone, and you'll observe their light and beauty inside. Your ability to connect and communicate with other people will increase your aptitude for achieving intimacy, understanding, and trust.

The Key to Healing Is to Release the Past

Conventional medicine suggests that we are healthy until a bacteria or virus makes us unhealthy, whereas in fact we come into contact with millions of germs every day with no apparent effect. Why is it, then, that not everyone is affected by these germs? How healthy were you when you were at the best point in your life—in love, or doing well financially, or simply enjoying being alive? And how quickly did you not feel well when your life seemed to be less easy?

The most important thing to realize is that *the quicker you release low-energy thoughts, low-energy words, and low-energy emotions, the healthier your physical body will be.* Your spiritual, emotional and mental condition then harmonizes and synchronizes to bring you fabulous success as you flow with life.

You are not the same person you were this time last year. Your body is the most wonderful mechanism. It replaces 95 to 98 percent of your cells annually. It regulates your temperature and sorts and carries hormones, enzymes, and nutrients to the perfect location at the correct time. It replaces your skin every month, your stomach lining every five days, your entire liver every six weeks, your whole skeleton every three months. The sixty-thousand miles of blood vessels transport blood cells (and new ideas) completely around your body every twenty minutes.

Fritz Alfred Popp at the University of Marburg in Germany proved that we use light stored inside the cells of the body to help us cope. Light is stored in the body by the DNA in the form of photons; stress, ill health, and depression increase the rate of biophoton emissions as a defense mechanism designed to bring the individual's energy back into balance. He proved that fresh, raw vegetables provide the most light. Meat, fish, and chicken provide secondhand light—not quite so appetizing when you put it like that, is it? Ideally, the healthiest body would be glowing with light—the nearest state possible to the source, or God.

I've always been able to see light around people, and when I see a healthy person, it looks like the person is surrounded by light. When someone is not healthy, or is depressed or on drugs, they appear to be surrounded by a gray (or even black) cloud. I was surprised once to see a man, who was a drug addict, with a ring of darkness almost half a yard thick enveloping his body. In other words, he had used up his supply of light from the body and was not at all well, as there was no more light for his cells to use to communicate with one another.

How do we get more light in our physical body? We do this with excellent nutrition (the fuel the body uses to convert to energy), especially any fruit or vegetable that's fresh and raw, by excellent thinking patterns and actions, and by regular "cleaning out" of the physical body.

Spring-Clean Your Body to Spring-Clean Your Mind

Our mind and body are part of one larger system that is in constant communication, each informing and influencing the other's well-being. I believe that if you are toxic on a physical level it interferes with the communication and thinking of the higher mind. Our ability to choose high-energy words internally and with others will be greatly enhanced when we also choose to treat our physical being with high-energy nutrients and care.

Every moment, year after year, your body and mind have worked well together to keep you healthy and alive in spite of low-energy patterns and habits. Although your whole body is made up of trillions of cells, every one of these cells has its own special job to do. What is most amazing about each cell is that its job is to work for the whole organism (the body). It "knows" what it has to do, even if it involves sacrificing itself for the greater good (as is the case with white blood cells).

Each cell "talks" to other cells via an electrical messaging system, which utilizes minerals and chemicals. These chemical messengers are called neurotransmitters. They bathe every cell in your body and are constantly eavesdropping on your nervous system, meaning that *when you have happy thoughts, you have happy cells.*

To keep my cells and my thoughts happy, I do a natural cleanse and go for a colonic (colon therapy to clear the intestines) once a month. I find that I have more energy and feel healthier and more connected as a result. Consult a qualified health practitioner, of course, if you decide to do any cleansing.

Having established really good communication between your body and mind, it's time to find out how to communicate with others for effective results. Communicating with others is so important because your relationship with others is your key to success at work or play.

I have been amazed to discover personally and with my clients that although most people believe that relationships are not easy, once you understand and learn how to make your physiology, tone, and words count, you can produce predictable results in relationships more quickly than in any other area of your life. For instance, how do you get someone to like you every time in sixty seconds or less? Read on!

Recap

1. Emotions are the messaging system your unconscious mind uses to let you know if you're on track.
2. Emotions are vitalizing, devitalizing, or neutralizing.
3. Your unconscious mind stores negative emotions in the body.
4. Every word has a chain of meaning that is interconnected with your neurology. Your cells are listening and responding.
5. "Like attracts like." Whatever you think and speak about will bring you more of the same.
6. Temporary change is easy. Establishing new behaviors is the key to permanent change.
7. People are not their behaviors. Everyone is doing the best they can with what they have available.

8. You have four bodies: a spiritual body, a mental body, an emotional body, and a physical body. They all need attention on a regular basis.

Chapter Five Action Plan

1. Get a glass of water and drink it now, or as soon as you can.
2. Make a note of what label you give to emotions as they come up. Write down a replacement word for any low-energy emotions and substitute that word when you talk about it. So, "I'm feeling angry" might become "I'm aware of some strong emotion that I need to clear."
3. Go to *www.YvonneOswald.com* and download the free recipe for the Gall Bladder and Liver cleanse. It's natural and easy (although it tastes not at all good).
4. Start a "Gratitude Book." Get an empty writing book that you can carry around with you, and make a note any time you feel grateful for something. Gratitude leads to optimism and keeps you in your "high brain."
5. Do fifteen minutes of exercise today. Simply reading about low-energy emotions will have triggered some interesting memories, and they need to be released or you'll have some amazing dreams tonight!
6. Pick a page in your day planner, sometime in the next month. Write at the top: "Great day! Fantastic day!" Think about it a lot, then wait and see what happens.

6

The Power of Communication and Understanding

To understand yourself faithfully and be understood
by others is to find peace in your spirit
and dwell in trust in your heart.

Thus far, we've explored how to understand yourself and the way your unconscious mind works in order to synchronize and harmonize your words and thoughts to have a great relationship with yourself. The next step is to take that knowledge and expand it so that your relationships with others are equally rewarding. Just imagine what it would be like to live on a planet where we all understand and accept one another!

You have, or have had in the past, a friend who liked (or loved) you unconditionally. This is the kind of friend who could push your comfort zones and you would still accept him or her. If your friend said "Jump!" you'd jump, and ask why later. This friend is someone you trust, someone you relate to, someone you can understand, validate, and empathize with. Wouldn't it be wonderful to have this bond with everyone?

Simply by learning some great behavioral skills, beginning with "rapport," this whole new world of connection is open to you. Do you remember that the language of words and symbols you use to talk to yourself accounts for 100 percent of your internal communication and results? Well, the language you use with others includes your body language and tonality. In fact, spoken words account for less than 10 percent of what you are actually communicating.

Frank is a client of mine. He is a highly qualified electrician in his late thirties. He is good-looking and intelligent. He's sensitive and caring, looks after his body, and owns two investment properties. Why then, could he not get past a first date with a girl? In working with him I discovered that he came from a very strict family background. He had been taught to stand straight, and stay quiet and still when someone else spoke; he had learned to override his natural instincts of interacting.

It took Frank only two hours of practice with me to learn simple body language patterns and voice tonality that brought amazing changes in his love life. He learned how to look at someone he found attractive, how to flirt in a respectful way, and how to appropriately touch someone he didn't know that well, but with whom he wanted to establish a closer bond.

He emailed me saying that he now finds these methods of adjusting his body language and tone of voice to interact with coworkers, as well as total strangers, amazingly practical. He recently met a girl in a store, and they ended up talking for half an hour. He says that even at the beginning stages of this new relationship, the part he used to find the least easy, he was able to feel comfortable. They are now dating and getting along wonderfully.

Before you discover how to direct your behavioral skills to expedite effective communication consciously, let's find out why rapport is so valuable.

The Language of Rapport

The language you use to perceive your intentions and convey them to others is called "rapport." Why do you need to know how to build rapport? What will it do for you exactly?

1. It increases your sense of self-confidence and charisma.
2. You can immediately make a great first impression, in both personal and professional situations.
3. You send out the right signals and become more interesting to other people.
4. You understand other people more easily and appreciate their model of the world.
5. Your attitude will change as you use your skills to become more welcoming and enthusiastic.
6. You increase intimacy levels in all your relationships.

As important as spoken language is, according to the study done in 1970 by Raymond Birdwhistle at the University of Pennsylvania, only 7 percent of communication is verbal. The other 93 percent is communicated unconsciously: 55 percent through body language and 38 percent through tone.

These "secret" language signals are often sent out and interpreted without your conscious knowledge, as your unconscious mind commands this whole area of communication. People will believe what your body is saying, rather than your words, if the two are at odds. For instance, if someone says "I really trust you" but at the same time shakes his or her head from side to side, you'll understand and believe the opposite of what they're saying (i.e., that they don't really trust you). At Harvard University, psychologists found that the attitude that students formed toward new teachers in the first two *seconds* of class remained the same throughout the course!

This is your chance to develop rapport at a conscious and unconscious level, enabling you to initiate the building of a lasting rapport in ninety seconds or less. Is that possible? Of course! Babies do it without the use of either language or tone. They instinctively match and mirror anyone who cares to put their face close; smiles are exchanged, eye contact is established, and touch is returned as baby squeezes your finger. A baby's very survival depends on people wanting to spend time with it. The "Aawww" appeal of a baby is no coincidence. Even before birth the fetus matches the body rhythms and functions of the mother. It is instinctive for children to mimic, particularly during their first seven years. This period is known as the "imprint" phase, when copying is a natural way for a child to learn about the world and relationships.

Studies show that eye contact during the first three months of life establishes the ability of an adult to achieve emotional intimacy. Babies who do not get close physical contact or eye contact, such as those born pre-term and put in an incubator or those who have a mother with few maternal instincts, will not find it easy in later life to establish close relationships or respond to intimacy.

Sharon came to me for help with her career. She was extremely likable and in a one-on-one setting had great communication skills. But in one work situation she was not so comfortable—at the weekly meeting of her coworkers and managers. She would pass out or throw up the second that attention was turned to her. She was also developing anxiety about anyone looking at her in other group situations—on the subway, for instance. This was not a fun way to live.

We looked for the root cause of this anxiety and found that Sharon had been born prematurely and was in an incubator for a long time. The only time anyone came to see her while she was in the incubator was to draw blood or do some tests. Those eyes on her at the weekly meeting lit up her stored internal and unconscious memories of those less happy times when she was much younger.

Sharon was able to realize and accept learning that those early treatments were not a threat but a lifesaving device, and that the nurses were her friends and there to help her. She phoned me with excitement the week following our appointment, and told me that she had thoroughly enjoyed the spotlight being on her at the business meeting and was very happy with the changes she had made.

It's up to us, as adults, to think carefully of the effect our words and actions may have on children. For example, a California study of toddlers, each of whom wore a tape recorder for a week, showed that whenever they were communicating with adults about anything, 85 percent of the time they were being told "No!"

Children who have parents with few communication skills, or children who have emotional interference patterns (which tend to lead to the child dissociating and disconnecting from others as a protection device), may find themselves "mismatching" his or her words, body language, or tonality without realizing. The other person feels uncomfortable around the mismatcher without knowing why and probably will avoid him or her in the future, confirming the mismatcher's belief that somehow he or she is not likable. The mismatcher's rhythms just don't match those of other people, so it may appear that the other person doesn't like them.

The more you are similar to other people the more they will like you. In fact, it's automatic when you meet someone new to establish common ground. You ask questions about his or her life, looking for something you can talk about together. When you find that something, the relationship takes a comfortable step forward. If you do not find commonality, you quickly move on. The simple fact is that you like people who are just like you.

We use our five senses to experience the world, through sight, hearing, touching, smelling, and tasting. The four main systems people use to process the information that's being received are visual, auditory, kinesthetic, and auditory-digital (self-talk); we call these our "representational systems." We each have one system or sense that tends to be more dominant. To determine your own predominant sense, ask yourself to recall the last time you took a vacation. What is it that stands out most for you about where you were? Was it the sights, the sounds, how you felt, what you were thinking, or what others said during your time there? (You can also go to my website and download the free test to determine your own representational system: *www.YvonneOswald.com*.)

Visually dominant people make up about 60 percent of the population. People who are primarily visual have an advantage over auditory or kinesthetic people in their ability to observe and copy postures, movements, and signals more easily. And because they tend to use eye contact more easily, they appear to be friendlier. However, we all use each of the senses, and our predominant sense may even change depending on the context of the situation.

If you are not as comfortable around other people as you would like, you can learn to increase your sensory acuity, using integrity and respect for others to create warm responses. You can learn the following rules and apply them with guaranteed success. Fake it until you make it, and then get ready to let go and let flow!

Like Me! Like Me!

We all seek approval: from our parents, friends, peers, and ourselves. Whether we know it or not, we instinctively want to be liked and accepted. Our survival used to depend on it, and sometimes still does, so it's wired into our neural pathways. You have much less than ten seconds to make that lasting first impression when you meet somebody new. Your job is to reassure the other person in the short term that you are safe to be around, and then to work on more enduring bonding if the relationship is worth continuing.

The first thing that someone will notice about you is how confident you are. Your number one key is to find and keep your power base. This gives you confidence and is a strong place to center yourself to make yourself feel good.

Magic of the Mind Nine

Power Base

First, find your belly button. Put three fingers underneath it as though you are patting your tummy; just below that is your power base, between your navel and your pubic bone. Simply bring your attention to that area now (eyes either closed or focused ahead and slightly upward), lift your chin slightly, hold your back straight, and breathe. You're instantly becoming calmer and more focused. Your power base is established simply by thinking a thought, and a brief intention is all that's needed to light it up.

To prove to you just how powerful this area is, do the following exercise with a friend. Have your friend stand with the back of his or her knees or calves against a really cozy armchair or comfortable couch (you're going to push your friend back onto it, so it needs to be supportive). Stand facing your friend, with your right shoulder to his or her right shoulder if you are right handed (or vice versa if you are a leftie). Your two shoulders should be about six inches apart. Place your right hand flat on their breastbone in the center of the chest and say: "I want you to stare over and above my shoulder with your eyes focused upward, and think of your left ear. Let me know as soon as you're there and I'm going to push you back onto the chair. As I do that, resist me as much as you can. Go ahead and think of your left ear now." It takes a fairly easy push to get them to sit down!

Have the friend stand up again and show them where to find their power base. Again, ask the person to look over your right shoulder, this time bringing their thoughts to the power base. It's amazingly different. Their resistance is powerful because they are so totally centered. I've easily pushed down a 250-pound man when he's thinking left ear, and found it not easy to push a ninety-five-pound woman when she's thinking of her power base!

A quicker version of this is to sit opposite a friend, and then ask your friend to talk to you while thinking of his or her left ear. Watch the eyes particularly. Then ask your friend to talk while his or her attention is in their power base. Notice how much more confident the person looks. In every situation, whether you're by yourself or meeting someone new, practice talking while thinking of your power base, and your confidence and energy will increase.

Meeting Someone New, Class 101

When meeting someone new, remember these five steps:

Step One—Confidence

1. Bring your attention to your power base.
2. Walk forward confidently. If sitting, simply sit straighter, or stand, as you turn your body to face the other person.
3. *Breathe,* and as you take that breath, raise your eyebrows briefly and open your eyes a little wider than normal. This eyebrow flash automatically makes the other person feel

welcome and acknowledged. You might also give a little half smile, as showing the teeth denotes friendship in Western culture.

4. Turn your body and head in the direction of the other person (a sign of respect), keeping eye contact as you do so (turning away implies nervousness or inferiority).

5. Lean in slightly toward the person as you show confidence and friendliness with a smile (preferably a wide smile or a series of brief, wide smiles if that makes you more comfortable).

Okay, so that's the first ten seconds covered. Yes, I do mean ten seconds!

Step 2—The Greeting

This is where you begin to observe the other person and go along with their model of the world. This is also the formal part of the ritual, which moves into words and touch. Part of being human means feeling closer to someone who touches you, so it's important that you reach out and take the other person's hand as you simply repeat their name (the old politician's trick). This has two effects:

1. It anchors the person's name and connects it to their face so that you remember who they are.
2. It makes the person feel important (people love to hear the sound of their own name).

The second time you meet someone, a brief touch on the upper arm (between the elbow and the shoulder) replaces the handshake and reestablishes familiarity and warmth.

Step 3—Matching and Mirroring

Our *physiology* is 55 percent of our communication. Matching and mirroring is how we notice our own physiology and make adjustments to it so that the other person feels more comfortable. It needs to be *subtle* so that the other person doesn't notice what you're doing and think that you're making fun of them.

- *Matching*—Match the other person's movements exactly. If he or she moves their right hand, you move your right hand a second or so later. If he or she crosses their legs, so do you.
- *Cross-over matching*—You match a behavior by crossing over into a similar movement with another part of your body. If someone crosses their legs, you cross your ankles. If someone is blinking rapidly, you might cross-over match by tapping your finger gently at the same rate.
- *Mirroring*—You mirror the other person's movements. If he or she move their left hand to their face, you move your right hand to your face, as though you are looking in a mirror.

If you are sitting down with the other person, sit at ninety degrees because that way you are not completely in their vision. Matching and mirroring needs to be just outside his or her awareness. You can match:

1. Posture—Adopt your physiology to this other persons. Are they leaning to the right or left? What is the angle of his or her spine, the tilt of their shoulders or head? Are the persons legs crossed? You might cross your ankles. This works well if someone's physiology is not friendly—if, for example, the persons arms are crossed. You could hold your hands with your fingers crossed together to modify their behavior.
2. Gestures—If someone touches their face or hair you can briefly raise your hand to your face a moment or two later. When it's your turn to speak you can copy this persons gestures. If they use large gestures, make yours large. If this persons gestures are small, tone yours down.
3. Facial expressions, smiles, and eye blinking—Match these expressions, including those of sadness, fear, or anger. Definitely match smiles briefly and copy blinking patterns, although you need to be careful with this one and only match if the blinking is in the normal range.

4. Match the persons breathing pace and the location of the breath—Are they deep or shallow breathers? People breathe out as they talk, so do the same with your breath.

You'll find very quickly that this is an amazingly powerful technique that deepens rapport. You'll also find that you begin to pace and lead the conversation as the other person begins to match and copy your movements.

Signs of Rapport

1. A feeling inside like "butterflies" or a quicker heartbeat
2. A color change in the face and neck of both yourself and the other person—a deepening or a flush
3. You find you both take turns leading and following body language automatically.
4. The other person may say something like: "I feel I've known you a long time," or "Haven't we met before?"

If you're not initially comfortable matching and mirroring, one of the easiest ways to gain rapport is to simply tip your head to one side and nod gently while maintaining eye contact. This movement shows that you approve of what the person is saying (always nice to know!) and that you're allowing the other person to dominate the conversation. If you wish to speed this person up, just nod faster and listen to how quick their language gets. They'll think you're fascinated and will go on and on. It's also natural to briefly look away and back during a conversation, so if your eyes begin to water you've probably held the gaze too long.

To get your turn to speak, turn your eyes away and back, assume a more upright posture, and perhaps take an obvious breath in as though you're about to speak. If the person still does not catch on, you might put up your index finger as though you're in class waiting your turn to answer a question. To close the conversation, nod your head as though bowing slightly, mismatch by moving your body posture as though you're about to leave, and make sure that as you speak your tone is in the form of a statement or command (down at the end): "It was great talking to you. Give me a call next week. Bye!"

Step 4—Match the Other Person's Voice

Tonality is 38 percent of communication. Matching the other person's voice is the quickest and most subtle way to gain rapport. When someone is introduced to you, the first word will probably be: "Hi," or "Hello," or "How do you do?" Match and echo the tone, speed, quality, and volume of their greeting *exactly* and your immediate acceptance is guaranteed. This is easiest to apply on the telephone, when you have no physiology to match. Practice by calling a friend and, as the friend answers, match his or her tone and words *absolutely*. The friend will know when it is right because he or she will feel more comfortable and may even say that you sound friendlier.

Another way is to sit back to back with someone and repeat something the person says with the same depth and resonance, like an echo. If you've got it right, he or she will feel much more comfortable. It's a small but important difference, rather like when you fold your arms one way and then fold them the opposite way. The right way just feels right.

Tone can convey a whole world of meaning. It can be conveyed three ways: as a statement—level voice; as a question—up at the end; and as a command—down at the end. When you reply to someone, use the same inflection on the last three or four words that was used with you. Match as closely as possible: the tone (pitch); tempo (speed)—the most important; timbre (quality); and volume (loudness).

Step 5—Language

Words are 7 percent of communication. In face-to-face situations, you can notice the physiology of another person to pick up communication clues, but on the phone, words need to convey more meaning. In auditory and nonvisual contexts, the importance of the words you use goes from 7 percent to 18 percent! This makes the phone a great place to practice your rapport skills because you'll then become a master wordsmith without also needing to pay attention to body language.

When someone picks up the phone, you have even less time to get approval than when speaking face to face since you are "judged" from your very first word. Practice matching each person's "hello" until it becomes automatic to reproduce it every time. You'll notice that some people talk slowly and some quickly. It's very important that even if it doesn't sound natural to you, you match their speed and tone. Usually, visual/auditory people tend to talk quickly and kinesthetic/self-talk people talk more slowly.

As a general rule, the representational systems people use to process information can be divided into four groups. A good way to remember is: look, listen, think, or feel.

1. Visual—They tend to talk quickly, have a higher-pitched voice, are less distracted by noise, and will respond to visual language such as "look" or "see."
2. Auditory—Their voice usually has more tonality (a bit like a radio announcer), they enjoy talking on the phone, they like music, and are more easily distracted by noise.
3. Auditory-digital—These are the people who self-talk. It has to be logical and make sense to these people for it to be understood. They think in sequences and like a step-by-step process.
4. Kinesthetic—They usually "feel" life by trusting with their gut instinct or feeling. They usually speak with slower, deliberate phrasing and use longer, more complex sentences.

Why is this important to understand? If you want to make yourself understood easily and quickly, you need to address someone using *his or her* dominant system for processing information. People simply do not find it easy to make sense of or relate to language that is not in their representational style.

Imagine living in a world where there are four different languages spoken, and no one bothers to learn the other three. Actually, you already do. In Western societies our educational system is set up to be primarily visual, and if your learning system is one of the other three, you may not have had an easy time understanding much of what you were being taught, particularly in spelling. For example, in spelling, kinesthetic children might access how they felt when a word was introduced to them, rather than seeing pictures of the letters or word. Auditory children might be trying to access the sound of the word instead of the picture. Many ADHD-diagnosed children today are simply using a different learning system than is commonly used in our schools.

Zak was a nine-year-old client whose mother brought him to see me. He was very angry, and had just been diagnosed with ADHD and put in a separate class. He appeared to be very bright and articulate; however he didn't make much eye contact. We chatted for a while and then I asked him what he thought of school. I commented that he seemed very clever. "I'm not clever. I've just been put in the dummy's class. I can't spell," he replied. I asked him to do me a favor so that I could help him by just imagining a safe place in nature. What would it be like? "That's easy. The birds are singing. The leaves are rustling. I can hear the sound of water and it's very peaceful and quiet." All the key words he used indicated that his learning system was auditory.

He closed his eyes and relaxed. His mom told him to open his eyes and look at me to connect. She repeated this over and over until I finally told her that it was fine with me that he didn't look, because his system was primarily auditory and he actually understood me better if he didn't have eye contact. He was processing what I was saying by listening, and although his eyes were closed, his ear was turned toward me.

Zak was delighted to know that he could overcome his apparent slowness by learning to read a book by holding it just above eye level and to the left (the area where we look for visual remembering), so that his visual recall pathways could be trained. I showed his mom how to do this by writing down the word "success" (written half in red and half in blue) and held it up and to the left of Zak's face, just above eye level, to teach him how to access the information correctly. I asked Zak to sound out the word. I gave him a clue and said that the second "c" sounded like "s." He got it fairly quickly.

Then I asked him to spell it out letter by letter, close his eyes, open his eyes, close his eyes and spell it. We had some fun by asking Zak to close, open, close, open, and then close his eyes and spell the word backward! He aced it and grinned broadly. His mom was amazed. I explained that her job was to remind Zak to use this fun method whenever he needed to learn a new word, and to teach him to hold the book just above eye level when learning new information. I also asked Zak to simply pretend to look at me instead of really looking at me. We connected for two very enjoyable hours. I used auditory language to talk with him and simply reminded him to pretend to look at me every now and again.

When they left, his mom was quite amazed that he'd stayed still and interested for so long. At one point as I gave him some positive suggestions, he was so relaxed his eyes were closed and he was almost asleep. His mom reported later that he was delighted to finally be understood and that she was doing her best to remember to use auditory words with him. His behavior also changed because he was no longer so frustrated.

My husband Will (auditory) and I (visual) used to not agree very much (that's an understatement, by the way) until we finally understood why we couldn't communicate well. We were each using our own representational systems to talk to each other. He would say, "Are you listening to what I'm saying?" and I would reply, "You're not seeing what I mean." We switched the sentences: he now says: "Do you see what I mean?" "Yes, I hear you," I reply, and it's as though we actually speak the same language at last.

Here are some examples of how you can use words to relate to others in speech:

Visual (V): *You're looking good. I see what you mean.*

Auditory (A): *I hear what you're saying. It sounds like you're listening.*

Auditory-digital (D) (Think of "self-talkers."): *I think you make total sense. I understand your thinking.*

Kinesthetic (K): *I sense that you're feeling good. I'm catching on.*

Simply by listening to the words that someone uses, you can quickly find out what their primary representation system is.

Notice one or two key words as they speak, and repeat them back in your own sentences. Once you've established rapport, you can ease off and they will still feel comfortable and connected with you. You'll be amazed by how quickly they appear to really like you.

There's a whole range of words you can and do use in each representational system. The list of predicates in the appendix will help you to become familiar with the sensory words favored by each representational system.

Language of the Eyes

You can quickly find out which representational system people use more predominantly by simply watching their eye movements. A Stanford University study of eye pattern movements in the late 1970s discovered that people move their eyes in accordance with whether they're seeing pictures, listening to sounds, accessing their feelings, or talking to themselves.

Visual people tend to make more eye contact and look up if you ask them to think about something as they picture it in their mind (they usually look up to their left, your right, as they're facing you). They usually take care of their appearance, as "looking good" is important to them. Normally, they have good posture and tense shoulders.

Auditory people find eye contact not so necessary. They often hold their head to one side without looking at you, as though listening. Their eyes might go horizontally back and forth from ear to ear as they "listen" inside. They love rhythm and often tap out a rhythm on a chair or table. You frequently see their lips move when they're thinking, as if they're talking to themselves. The stereo is always on at home or in the car.

Auditory-digital (self-talk) people look down to your right when you speak to them as they talk to themselves and decide how to respond. They can sometimes appear a bit dissociated and stiff, as they live in their heads more than most.

Kinesthetic people look down to your left as you look at them; they are accessing how they feel about things. They tend to be rounder, more relaxed individuals with fuller lips and a body posture that leans in a round-shouldered way. They breathe more deeply and have a relaxed manner and a deep voice. They choose clothes for comfort rather than fashion.

When you use the person's own model or way of experiencing the world, communication is smoother and you can establish rapport very quickly. The other person feels that you know them at a very deep level and will remember you. In business these concepts are proving to get some great results. Debra Burns, the founder and managing director of Boss Model Management, the largest modeling agency outside London, England wrote this to me:

I just thought I'd drop you a line with a bit of feedback on your great new methods. After completing the exercises myself and then introducing them to my staff, the results are already proving beneficial in relations between staff internally (sometimes very fraught in this extremely fast-paced and frenetic environment), and also with the models we are working with on a day-to-day basis.

We have used the ideas in workshops too—workshops are held free of charge and are available to all the new relationships we are developing. There is so much common sense in the language switching. I can't believe that this is a totally new concept, and for me the sooner it takes off the better! ALL the people involved are clearer in their communication and are more confident as a result because they understand themselves (models can be challenging to get to know). As a result, they are suddenly succeeding in castings when auditioning for jobs. I know there are loads of self-help type books and guides available, but your idea really shines out and you deserve all the recognition for it. It is concise, to the point, and it works.

From here on you'll find the dramatic changes in your thinking and behavior beginning to pay off. It's time to language yourself happy as we go on to discover how to super-boost your life by putting the concepts to work in the areas of personal relationships and goal setting.

Recap

1. You already have all the resources you need for effective communication.
2. The response you get from others is based on how you convey your meaning.
3. The four representational systems people use to process information are: visual, auditory, auditory-digital and kinesthetic (see, hear, think, feel).
4. Communication is 7 percent words, 38 percent tonality, and 55 percent body language.
5. People believe your unconscious signals more than the words you speak.
6. Head to one side, nodding, is always friendly.
7. When we all understand ourselves and others, we'll have world peace.

Chapter Six Action Plan

1. Call a friend and practice matching their tone of voice and the words they are using, without letting them know what you're doing.
2. Smile at everyone you meet today (and every day).
3. Highlight three words from each list in the Representational System Predicates table (see appendix) that you feel comfortable using, and then practice them.
4. Go to *www.YvonneOswald.com* and print out the Representational System Test in "Great Free Info" to discover your own representational system.
5. To find a family member's representational system, listen to the words they use. Then talk to them using their own words, and observe the difference in the response you get.
6. Think of your power center right now, and breathe a deep breath of energy into it.

7

The Power
of Relationships

To love another person is to see the face of God.
—Jean Valjean in *Les Miserables*

Relationships are the food of life. Even if you came from a dysfunctional family (and who didn't?), the responsibility for the success of all of your relationships lies with you. Your family is the product of a series of inherited patterns: the negative ones that you can choose to observe and change, and the positive patterns that you can grow and make stronger. Relationships outside of your upbringing are 100 percent of your choosing. So the question is this: are you nourishing yourself by surrounding yourself with healthy connections, or are you still visiting that old empty relationship café?

Wonderful relationships are about giving and receiving affection, warmth, understanding, acceptance, love, kindness, sweetness, hugs, entertainment, fun, sincerity, truth, integrity, intelligence, honesty, and trust, as well as having respect for yourself and everyone you meet. Being loved and understood allows you to feel validated and worthy. The value you place on every moment of your life is reflected in the type of people you surround yourself with at work and in your home setting. In reality, your relationships *are* your home. They are your healing garden and your sanctuary.

In life, energy is always being exchanged, mostly outside your conscious awareness. In a relationship, you can actually feel the energy exchange because you feel good, or not so good, when you're in the company of another person. In your relationships, you have the strongest emotional links, so the words you use are loaded with possibilities for amazing, or not so amazing, results. Be prepared to open your mind and grow, and learn to think and speak in a supportive way toward everyone around you. The best relationships are those that allow you to be free to be yourself.

The wonderful thing about relationships is that every person you meet is showing you how well-connected you are with your unconscious or inner mind, because you can only notice qualities in other people that you have resolved, or not resolved, in yourself. Those people and encounters that you allow to "get to you" are the ones that give you your best lessons. If you use the experiences wisely, you'll realize that what you gain is a gift that leads to a better solution, and to feeling good about yourself and the other person. In chapter two you found out that what you most like about others is what others most admire about you. Now it's time to find out how far you can stretch yourself.

Everyday Words ... Exciting Results

When you use low-energy words, the person you are speaking to quickly begins to associate you with those words. For example, if I were to say to someone: "I'm not criticizing you ("criticize" being a low-energy word), just trying to understand," their unconscious immediately associates me with "criticize," and will continue to do so.

When I use high-energy words, I also change my tonality, and the person quickly changes their feelings about me in response. For example, if I were instead to say to someone, "That's great.

Please explain to me how it works," their unconscious then associates me with "great" and the feelings that go with "great."

Rose-Anne wrote to me after a private session, saying that she'd quickly realized once she returned home how her internal and external language patterns were actually creating more stress in her life. Her first step toward changing this was simply to notice, or give more attention to, how often she chose nonsupportive words in her day-to-day speech. With practice and patience, a simple positive shift in her vocabulary (by using "switch" as a game) greatly improved her family life with her children and her husband. When she reverted to her low-energy language and said something like, "Don't talk to me like that," her daughter would tell her to "switch," and she'd respond with high-energy words: "Thank you for lowering your voice." She and her daughter were able to find solutions following such shifts, rather than further misunderstanding.

Another benefit was that when she switched her words in her business relationships, her sales and profits started to soar. Her sister is a teacher, and used the principles of high-energy thinking and speaking in the classroom. She, too, reports great success, saying that there is now a happier and more open atmosphere among her students.

A client, Daniel, is a business president in the field of health and fitness videos. He is a sunny and unassuming person, and, although good at his job, wanted something more fulfilling in his career. When he applied the switch principles to his language, he also found that the positive effects motivated him to switch his outlook on life. He started his own company, which he had secretly dreamed of doing, and became so skillful using the switch patterns that he gained the confidence and the ability to present his ideas and business concepts successfully to colleagues and clients. As a result, his business took off and continues to thrive, and Daniel is achieving his potential, enjoying his creativity, and moving ever closer toward his goals.

You can use each of the strategies we've covered so far to make all of your relationships work well. It's time to connect with everyone in an easier and more comfortable way. The need to connect is basic; common to animals and humans, males and females, rich and poor. Part of being human is the need to feel integrated and aligned with universal and corporeal love. Why is it, then, that we sometimes feel like we don't belong or are not attached?

My theory is that to some extent, we all have areas of our character that look like this, a pie that's not yet complete:

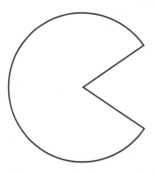

FIGURE 1

Now, *like attracts like*, remember? All you can attract when your pie is not complete is another pie with a piece missing:

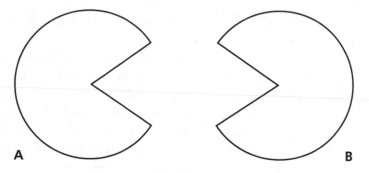

A   B

FIGURE 2

Hands up, all you caretakers or caregivers!

In the diagram above, "A" (the caretaker) says: "I recognize you! You're just like me! (Or, more simply put, "I really like you!") Let me help you fill that hole with love, care, cooking, and so on. I'll organize your bank balance, help you get a job, or change hats to be whatever you want me to be."

"B" (the receiver) says: "Thanks very much!" Unfortunately, B's incompleteness is only going to be filled temporarily from A's ministering since we can only be truly complete from within, not from without. Also, to fill B's circle, A has to use some of her own circle. The result?

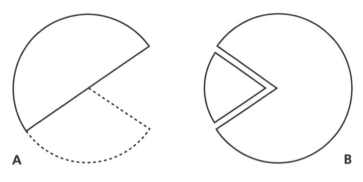

A   **B**

FIGURE 3

This is a picture of how codependency happens. "A" feels better when she's with B because B has her stuff (i.e., all the time and effort spent trying to make the relationship work and make B complete). "A" does not feel good when she's apart from B.

Aristophanes, the Greek comic and poet, said that each person is half of a single unit of love and that the goal is to find the other half. I don't believe that's true. When we each complete our own circle, we can then attract someone else who is also a complete circle. Thus, this figure is also the symbol for infinity, and the number eight, which in numerology is the number of power, money, success, and self-worth. It's time for you to learn to be a good receiver, too.

Surprisingly enough, it's been proven that if you are having a less than easy time with someone, doing something nice such as getting a coffee or complimenting them makes you feel more friendly toward them. A friend who was also a colleague was sympathetic when a client was proving to be very bold in a class I

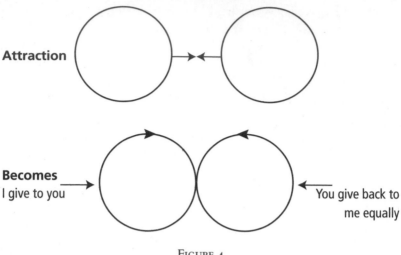

Attraction

Becomes
I give to you

You give back to
me equally

FIGURE 4

was teaching. I told the friend that I was really attempting to find something nice about the client that I could focus on. She said quite genuinely, "She has really nice hair." It made me laugh so much that I was able to see the funny side of the situation and welcome the client as someone who was doing her best. I smiled at the client, and she immediately began to loosen up.

Relationships: Time and Timing

A number of years ago, there was a wonderful advertisement on the television: Miss Smith was walking along the street, loaded up with parcels. Mr. Jones was at right angles to her, just about to cross the street. The ad then showed the future; he was going to bump into her, take her for coffee by way of an apology, marry her, live in a lovely house, have two great children, and live happily ever after. Then it reverted to the present and the anticipation of the meeting. The ad soundtrack was a bit like *Jaws* as Mr. Jones approached Miss Smith: ("Dah duh, dah duh, dah duh, dah duh!"), and just as he reached her, he went right behind her and into a shop doorway. At the end of the ad the announcer said, "He should've been wearing a Timex watch!"

That describes *exactly* how relationships work. We either meet the right person at the right time, or it isn't the right person or the right time. When we're in a relationship that isn't working, we need to trust the "just missed" effect and move on, instead of giving it six weeks, six months, six years, or six lifetimes! We've all at some point hung around in the shop doorway, waiting for an unsuitable person instead of moving on.

Remember that you have a quantum nature, and this means that you are connected at subspace level with everyone and everything. To see this in action, take a few minutes to watch a group of people sitting in a conference, at work, in a lecture, or even in a bar or restaurant. Notice how many of them suddenly start matching and mirroring each other's body language. One person will cross his or her legs, and pretty soon others will do the same. One may touch their face and so will the rest. They may not even know each other, and yet you'll see this chain reaction happen. So, is it possible to connect with the energy of someone you've not yet met and ask both your unconscious minds to find each other? I believe that it is.

If you've not found your partner, or simply want to reconnect with the one you've got, this visualization works very well. First of all, choose the exact date that you'd like to have your dreams come true (be somewhat realistic here). Then do the following exercise:

Magic of the Mind Ten

Allow yourself to get into a comfortable position with your back straight. Close your eyes. Imagine yourself floating above your body. Float forward to the exact date that you want your dreams to come true. As you stand above the event, observing yourself below with the love of your life, imagine going down into the picture into your body, and really feel the event happen. Turn up the colors; turn up the sounds, thoughts, and feelings. Imagine the emotions strong and powerful, and feel that "click" as you hug or hold your love.

Where are you? Who else is there? Is it a celebration, or are you alone with your partner? Feel the smiles inside, and when you can almost taste the feeling, float up above the picture and observe yourself and your partner in love and happy below. Breathe four powerful breaths into the picture to give it life, and then click your fingers to lock it into the place and the time you have chosen.

Turn and face back to now, still floating above the picture. Ask your unconscious mind (or God, if you prefer) to align and realign all the events from now to then, and then to now, to support your having everything you want. Observe a shaft of sunlight whooshing you back to the present. Then float back to now and open your eyes.

The Marriage Connection

Why is it that we have a deep need to marry or make a promise to stay with someone? Because you marry your unconscious mind. Let me repeat that: you marry your unconscious mind. That means that any area of your life that is not in harmony will surface the further you go into a marriage, in order to be worked through and cleared.

I use the word "marriage" to mean a commitment or a union between two people, including common-law situations and gay relationships. Marriage is an honoring of the other person and a sharing of mutual goals for the benefit of both people involved. Marriage, to me, is a sacred promise. When we start talking about petty things, my husband Will reminds me, "We promised on our wedding day that we wouldn't do this." It brings me up short and takes me immediately back to that lovely day when I felt like a princess.

So, how do you keep the marriage alive and growing through the years? As a place to start, determine the representation system your partner uses. Is she or he more visual, more auditory, or more kinesthetic? Quite often, communication challenges are as simple as your partner using a different sensory filter from yours.

When you can both understand and use this awareness in your communication, the relationship becomes a whole lot easier.

Another important component is to make sure that you each have outside interests and a sense of purpose in life, both individually and jointly. Keeping a sense of humor is essential too. The word to always keep in mind when you're talking to your partner is "kind." If you are anything less than that, unpleasant emotions will surface faster than a flash flood.

Dr. Carrie Bailey, a psychologist and counselor, had been having challenges in her marriage. She didn't realize that her husband was auditory-digital, so she had been telling him of her feelings and what she could see happening in their relationship—and not getting very far. When she started to talk about what made more sense to her and asked him what he thought about things, it was as though he lit up. She wrote to me, saying:

Being aware of my language has transformed my life in unexpected ways. It has shown me where I need to heal. I learned that any unpleasant thought I had came with a corresponding unpleasant feeling. As I consciously began to change my thoughts, my feelings toward my husband grew more loving and accepting. It felt like my heart was expanding and I saw him through compassionate eyes. Our interactions became more positive because he was open to using the same tools. Happily, we have fallen in love all over again.

Praise and Validate

In that first flush of love, we praise, praise, praise! We say, "I like you because you're so handsome and talented. You're great with people, you know. I love being with you." With time, this can turn into, "It's your turn to take out the garbage. Oh, and you could move those socks and shoes you left in the hall on your way out. Thanks."

Here's a communication exercise you can use. When you're alone together ask, "What do you still like about me?" (If the partner says, "I like . . . , but" tell him or her to edit the "buts"—pure praise please!) This question asks your partner to remember why he or she chose to be with you in the first place, instead of thinking about what you're *not* doing. If you feel sometimes that you are not communicating fully, say something nice to your partner instead of anything else that was about to come out. This is not easy sometimes, I know! It does open doors, however. The person in the relationship who has the most flexibility will always lead it toward growth.

There's also a wonderful technique called the "Feedback Sandwich." Tell the person with whom you want better communication the following:

1. What you like/love about the person or what you think they do well
2. What you'd like to have happen to make you feel more supported
3. That overall, the job they're doing is great and you really appreciate it

This works wonderfully with coworkers, children, family, and friends. You'll find out how effective this is when they take your comments as a compliment and change just the way you want them to!

In order for a relationship to continue to work, two things need to happen. First, your feelings about the other person need to stay positive, and the love strategies of both partners need to remain fulfilled. You should both know what to do or say to make the other person feel loved. How do you find that out? You simply ask what's important to them about love and intimacy. Get specific with this one. It's the small things that make a difference.

And secondly, if the relationship really isn't working, if one of you has grown away or the resentment is too deep, give it a "sell by" or "best before" date, and *tell* the partner first. "I'm really not happy with our relationship. Do you want it to continue like this, or are you willing to work with me to see if we can improve it by this summer/Christmas/Hanukkah?" Putting it in an actual time frame implies that the relationship will be reviewed or finished by that date, so that both of you can move on.

The best marriages I have seen are those where each partner delights in the other's accomplishments and achievements. The phrase usually begins: "I am so proud of him (or her) because...." We are always proud and easily boast about our children. It would be lovely to validate our marriage relationships the same way.

Children—The Treasure of the World

Your children are not your children.
They are the sons and daughters of Life's longing for itself.
They come through you but not from you.
And though they are with you they belong not to you.
You are the bows from which your children as
living arrows are sent forth.
—Kahlil Gibran, *The Prophet*

Our children hold the key to the future of humanity, and it is by teaching them how to communicate well in relationships that you can ensure their happiness. The famous singer Celine Dion appears to have it all: looks, money, success, romance, and fame. And yet, she says that if there's a secret to happiness in life, having a child is that secret.

For me, it's a privilege to be a parent, and one I truly appreciate because I had to wait so long to have a child. I talked to my daughter from the moment she was conceived (actually, it was probably *before* that). I would walk in the sunshine and tell her about the breeze I could feel against my face. I would get in the bath and splash water noisily, and tell her how much she would love the water (she adores it). I did some therapy to prepare for the birth and release any anxiety.

When she was four years old I asked her casually if she remembered being born.

"Yes, it was dark and then it was light."

"Do you remember the nice music that was playing?" I asked.

"No, but I remember it smelled *lovely*. My bum was *really* sore for three days. And I remember daddy talking." Katie was a frank breech at birth, so her bottom was black and blue; amazing that she somehow knew.

Children remember a great deal between three and four years old. The "new" personality then begins to integrate, and the memories fade. Katie has no recollection of her birth now. However, I would always talk to Katie—even when she was a baby—as though she understood everything I said. Remember that your unconscious mind is listening and making notes. It believes that everything you tell a child is something that you believe about yourself. Make it different and make a difference.

We Are the Keepers of the Sacred Space

Every child believes that their dreams will come true. Can you create the words that may lead a child to believe that they learn amazingly fast, or that their ideas are great, or that they made some superb choices? Can you view a child's every action as an interesting behavior? Can you simply ask "For what reason?" when a child acts out, and find humor in the situation? Focus on the act, not the child, and support and look for a solution without punishment. Punishment usually arises out of low-energy thoughts and words, and simply "anchors" the low-energy behavior in the child even further. Ask the child what he or she could do differently to get a happier result. Children know. They are in touch with deep inner wisdom.

Eventually, enough low-energy experiences and instructions can impact the way a child (and later the adult) thinks about and responds to life. The low-energy voice inside is the inner dialogue that interferes with success because it blocks the communication channel from the source of abundance. The less happy someone is, the more fragmented and unstable they become, drifting further away from what they want to have, be, or do.

It is with our children that we have the chance to change the world to make it a happier place. In my therapy sessions, I have taken hundreds of people back to before birth, back to the moment of conception. When asked what lesson they are to learn, the client's answers are simple:

- "To love and be loved."
- "To be self-reliant."
- "To care for others."
- "To learn to receive."
- "To overcome."
- "To learn that life's not always easy."

To achieve their full potential as adults, our children need to be loved and accepted completely by parents who love themselves and each other. Happiness and self-worth are all about love.

The chart on page 152 shows the progression of love in children or adults, the left side showing positive and high-energy movement, and the right side showing the opposite. Words are so important!

"Safe Place" Exercise

Nighttime is sometimes not easy for a child, as children have such fertile imaginations. They are more connected to the unconscious mind, so the mind releases daily emotional buildup more quickly and easily. Establish this five-minute exercise as a routine so that you get a good night's sleep.

Hold the child's hand and say softly:

Close your eyes. Let's pretend.
Alright, we're going to find a safe place in nature for you to go. Would you like a seaside and beach, a mountain, a lovely forest of trees, or a tree house in the garden? Tell me about the place. Imagine the birds singing, the sun shining warmly on your skin. Can you hear any water? See how clear the colors are. Is there someone to play with? Who else is there? Are there any animals? What's happening now?

Make as few suggestions as you can to detail the scene because the child should use his or her own creativity and imagination (and representational system) as much as possible. Children will normally go to the same place again and again, and replay the same scene over and over with just small variations.

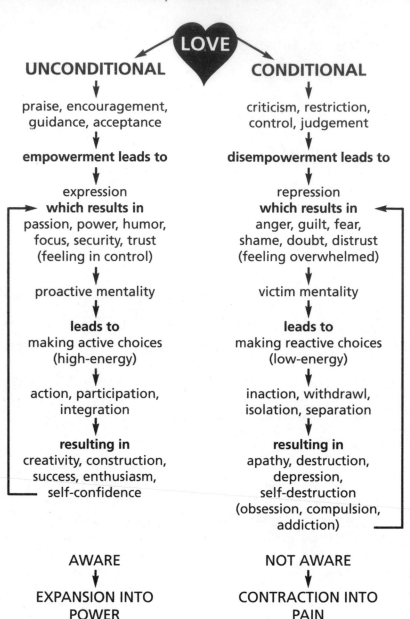

FIGURE 5

152

Dreams can also be scary experiences for children. Once you've established the five-minute "safe place" as a ritual, you can get the child to go there immediately if a disturbing dream occurs. Ask your child to describe the least happy part of the dream (e.g., a monster), and then ask how he or she thinks you can make it go away together. You might say, for example, "Should we get Super Dog to come and take it away? Shrink it into a small box? Put it on a boat and send it out to sea?" Use your imagination. This teaches a child to use theirs, and find an immediate solution to a scary or uneasy situation, which in turn will give the child great coping tools for later in life. You can also teach Magic of the Mind Six from a very early age.

Recap

1. Free yourself to be yourself.
2. Clear nonsupportive relationships from your life after deciding what the lesson was: let go and move on.
3. The one valid emotion in a relationship is love, expressed with warmth and kindness. If a negative emotion shows up, it simply means that you are ready to learn something more about yourself.
4. You marry your unconscious mind and project onto your children everything that you've not yet cleared away from your past.
5. As parents, our job is to guide and help to teach our children to manage the strong emotions and feelings that accompany childhood.
6. The most amazing people are out there searching for you, just as you are searching for them.
7. If you do something nice for someone, it helps you to like them more.

Chapter Seven Action Plan

1. Give everyone you meet a warm smile today, especially strangers. You may make a real difference in their life.

2. Greet everyone you meet as though they are an adorable puppy, with a smile on your face. Smile while talking on the phone. Pretend that everyone is your best friend for a day.

3. Fill in a page of your gratitude book with people you like and the reasons you are grateful that you know them.

4. Do the Ho'oponopono Forgiveness Exercise (in the appendix) every day for a week to improve your relationships. Do Magic of the Mind Six to release old relationships.

5. Time how long, as a percentage of the day, your partner or children are not well behaved or pleasant. Then be happy and celebrate that it's not very long after all.

6. Give everyone you know a compliment when you see or hear them.

7. Have fun with the person (or persons) you love the most today.

8

The Power of Spiritual Connection

*You can only receive presents from God
when you're in the presence of God.*

The Power of the Spirit—Human Energy

Spiritual health is vital to your well-being because having an awareness of something greater than yourself allows you to be at peace in your heart. It makes you feel deeply connected.

How can you connect with and harness the power of the spirit so that you can direct the energy into channels of creativity and manifestation? All you are and all you see, feel, hear, or touch is energy. You yourself are simply a rainbow of energy fields, a dance of light and shadows. The energy forms different degrees of speed and density, and it diffuses throughout and outside of your physical body. Energy can never be erased; it simply changes its form. Your physical, mental, and emotional body takes in universal energy through the top of your head, although the energy connection is more like a matrix than a channel since every part of your physical body has space between each quantum particle. Hence, you are intricately connected on a quantum level with everything and everyone in the universe.

What is important to recognize is that the healing of the spiritual body is a "do with" not a "do to" process. Spiritual harmony is achieved by recognizing that there is something more to life than what your five senses tell you. It's the development of the sixth sense, the higher consciousness that takes you to a new level of understanding. The name we usually give to that sixth sense is the unconscious mind. It's an awakening from within. It connects you to God.

Spiritual health is about learning to trust, even when you feel you have reasons not to trust. It's about opening yourself up to the idea of understanding that the positive lesson is there and will be revealed over time. Sometimes simple acceptance is more powerful than any amount of questioning.

Albert Einstein said that a man's experience is an optical delusion of his consciousness, meaning that what we perceive to be "reality" is totally subjective and that we delude ourselves into believing otherwise. You might think of this as though you—the *real* you—is looking at yourself in a mirror. The "you" that is looking back at you from the glass is not real, although it looks as though there is someone else there. Have you ever watched a small child catch sight of his reflection and then go around the back of the mirror to look for the other child? Sometimes as adults it's good to remember that fear, low-energy emotions, and limiting beliefs are illusion, too.

Our low-energy voice, which is accompanied by low-energy emotions such as anger, sadness, fear, and guilt, and limiting decisions and beliefs, comes from our unconscious mind. Our unconscious is also how we connect to our spiritual feelings and words. Removing low-energy thoughts and feelings from this stream of connection allows us to access and dialogue with the inner or real person, who is naturally in balance and harmony. Using life-affirming words connects you with the high-energy voice and the true voice inside, thus making a quantum leap forward to access abundance and joy on every level.

Carl Gustav Jung's study of primitive tribes led him to believe that there is a vast, hidden store of images common to all of humankind, regardless of race or creed. He called this the *collective uncon-scious*: a storehouse of knowledge that can be "tapped" by tuning in to a higher frequency than normal.

Rupert Sheldrake, the British biologist and author, discovered that self-organizing living things—from molecules to entire galaxies—are shaped by *morphic fields*; they have morphic resonance. What this means is that every time you learn something, it is immediately passed on to the rest of humanity, rather like a cumulative and collective memory. This explains how two scientists can, and often do, discover something at two different places on the planet at the same time. This is also where dynamic excitability comes in. Knowledge is passed at a high level, so if two keen individuals are focused on the same quest, then one person's knowledge will impact the other's and vice versa. If the two strangers have no common interest, then the subsequent reaction will be small, not enough to cause conscious awareness.

Let's take a look at how we connect and interact with one another from a quantum spiritual perspective using the diagram below. Imagine two strangers who will never meet. Their actions will be recorded on a higher level, or higher vibration, than their awareness, in the space we call the collective unconscious or super conscious (also known as the Akashic Records) and of course, on a higher level still, God, or the Universal Mind.

Two Strangers

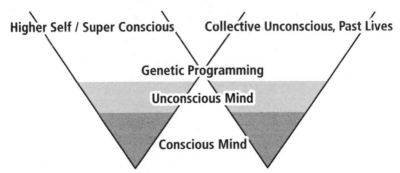

FIGURE 6

Family members share the same genetic space/collective unconscious space and universal space. While two of them may both have red hair, they may have little else in common. However, if they both have emotional issues and one person does therapy to release the low-energy emotions, subsequent generations sharing the same genetic coding will benefit by having the low-energy memories erased from the genetic material.

I know from the regression work I've done with clients that by experiencing the memory and releasing it, we also clear the residual genetic patterning (like clearing out a virus), meaning that our own children will be free from this particular pattern. This "genetic memory" imprint can also contribute to "false memories" that are uncovered by some regression work, as perhaps some long-forgotten *genetic* memories surface and are mistaken for current life memories.

Close Family Members/Friends
Daily Contacts/Workmates

God / Universal Mind

Higher Self / Super Conscious,
Collective Unconscious, Past Lives,
Genetic Programming

Unconscious Mind

Conscious Mind

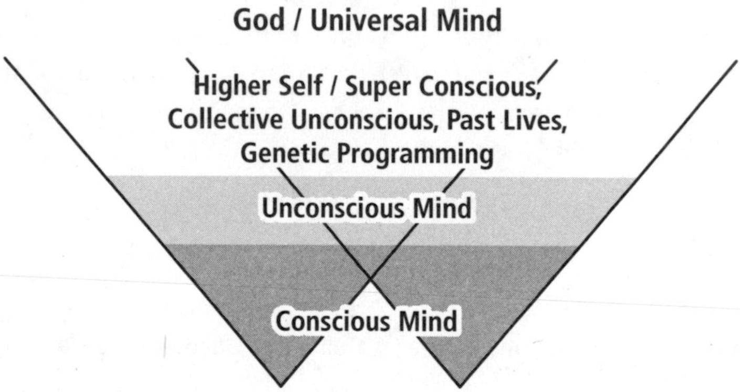

FIGURE 7

Close family members/friends/daily contacts/workmates can also share conscious and unconscious, as well as the collective/upper and universal unconscious. This explains why the people you meet on a physical level, whether simply as acquaintances, coworkers, or lovers, act as your mirror!

By sharing the same physical space, you observe your own least and best qualities, explaining why you love people who are just like yourself and why you can dislike intensely someone who is just like yourself!

Just Breathe and Go Within

Meditation is considered to be a spiritual practice because it quiets the thoughts and allows us to connect with our higher conscious mind. When you meditate, find a quiet place in your home to do it. As far as body position is concerned, the only thing to remember is to keep your back straight so that the energy centers are aligned. If your home is not always tidy, have at least one area of your home that is tidy and spacious so that you can feel free to just relax there. With practice, meditation will clear the channels for you to switch your language easily and joyfully.

Here's a quick and easy meditation exercise:

Sit with your back straight and your head erect, as though someone is pulling it up with a rubber band. Imagine a beautiful sun, or the light of God, shining clearly above your head. Inhale to the count of seven, breathing in the universal light energy through the top of your head. Hold the breath and count to seven, imagining the golden rays of light flowing into your heart center (the middle of your chest). Then exhale to the count of eleven, pouring out the energy in a golden stream of light, expanding from your body to the stars.

To obtain the optimum state of wellness while you are in this meditative state, imagine a holographic image of yourself standing on a platform in front of you. If you wish, you can imagine this image on a computer screen. Now observe the image turning around as though on a turntable. Notice that it is exactly like you want to be: perfectly healthy, slim, strong, and fit. Breathe four breaths of light energy into every cell of your holographic body as you feel, see, or imagine the body aligning itself with the blueprint of perfect health and functioning. If you notice any areas that are less than bright, imagine a light laser zapping and clearing those areas. Think of an exact date sometime in the next few days or in the next month when you know that it will be possible for you to look like the image in front of you; write it somewhere under or over the image. Make sure you include the day, month, and year.

For spiritual healing, to connect with yourself on a deeper level, repeat over and over in prayer, just before sleep:

"I place it in the hands of God." ("It" being whatever the issue is!)

"I place myself in the hands of God." (You can replace "God" with "the universe," or whatever word works for you.)

"I am one with the source."

You may also want to increase the energy physically by tapping your thymus area (in the center of your chest, just below the collar bone) with your eyes closed, while thinking of a time when you were very happy or of someone you love. Breathe. The tapping opens the energy channels. Then place your left hand flat over the thymus, right on top of left. Imagine your heart opening like a flower and expanding pink energy to reach both hands. Breathe.

Meditation/Visualization to Clear and Balance Your Energy

Record the following into a tape recorder, then replay it, close your eyes, and listen:

 Imagine a beautiful spring day. You are alone in a cabin in the woods by a calm blue lake, surrounded by trees and mountains. The air is crisp and clean. There's a fire burning in the grate, and you can smell the wood smoke. It's a cheerful, comfortable place.

Feel the warmth of the fire on your face and body. Watch as the red flames flicker around pine logs, and smell the rich scent of the pine as they are consumed by the red fire. Feel the heat relaxing your body, and take a deep breath of the red energy of the fire. Take the red to a small spot at the base of your spine, and breathe out the rest.

Find a basket of oranges on the hearth next to the fireplace. Pick up one of the oranges and feel its round, rough skin. Dig your fingers deep into the flesh and smell the fresh essence. Feel the juice drip down over your hands and fingers, and suck the juice down into your body to a place just below your navel. Leave a small spot of orange energy there, and breathe the rest out.

Stand up and walk toward the door of the cabin. As you open the door, the bright morning sunlight streams in. Feel its warmth on your face, and take a deep breath of the yellow sunlight. Breathe the light down to your solar plexus, between your ribs and above your navel. Imagine the yellow energy expanding throughout your body as you continue to breathe in the light.

Find yourself walking down to the lakeshore along a path. The trees on either side of the path are just sprouting new green shoots. As the trees diminish and you come to a clearing in the front of the lake, new spring grass greets you. Breathe the green into the center of your chest, leave a small spot of green there, and breathe out the rest.

As you look up at the sky, the pink streaks of morning are still clearing. Breathe in the pink, and take it to the very center of your chest, inside the green. Leave a small spot of pink there, and breathe out the rest.

Blue water. Blue sky. A breathtaking view of mountains in the distance, towering over the majestic blue lake, gleaming in the morning sunshine. Breathe in the blue, listen to the birds sing, and take the blue energy to a place in the center of your throat. As you breathe out the rest of the blue, breathe the word "Haaah!"

Become aware of the beauty of the purple mountain across the lake, and take a deep breath of purple energy from it deep into your lungs and up to your forehead. Breathe out the remainder of the purple energy. As the sun climbs in the sky, sit down by the lake and

> *absorb the beauty of nature—the feeling of oneness with the universe. Relax, let everything go, and just be in the moment as you sit on a rock or a log, feeling the presence of a greater power.*
>
> *Mist rises from the lake and surrounds the base of the trees, winding its way softly around your feet. Take a deep breath of the mist; breathe it up to the top of your head in a counterclockwise direction, then release it with a deep sigh. You are one with truth, beauty, and knowledge. With peace in your heart, open your eyes to a brand new day.*

It's time. Now that you've discovered how your inner mind works, found your self-worth, cleared out old emotional interference patterns, cleaned out your physical body, and learned about how to communicate with yourself and others, your connection with spiritual abundance is complete. Now let's put it all together as you activate that dynamic excitability to manifest everything you ever wanted in the material world.

Recap

We are all one. Everything you say, do, or think has an impact on you, me, and the rest of humanity, like ripples in a pond.

Chapter Eight Action Plan

1. Be very kind to yourself today (and every day).
2. Imagine an energy connection like a golden cord going out to every person you think about or meet. Send them an imaginary bright light, and wish them well. Your unconscious mind will believe that it's also meant for you and will return it like a gift.
3. Paint a room in your home in a beautiful color. Rearrange the furniture so that it feels wonderful and restful, like a sanctuary.
4. Sign up right now for a creative course; learn painting, meditation, pottery, or dancing. This is the time to begin doing what you've wanted to do for a long time.

9

The Power to Change the World

God does not play dice with the universe.
—Albert Einstein

New Words, New Key to Your Destiny

It's time . . . to affect change in every part of the world, beginning with yourself. By clearing your thought and speech patterns, your life choices will increase as though by magic. It's time to make a difference now, because every word you speak and every thought you think is resonating and vibrating throughout the world. It is on some level affecting every person on the planet. As you create your words, you create your (and our) destiny.

Once everyone realizes that by speaking, thinking, and acting clearly and with high-energy intent, the quantum possibilities of the development of the neocortex can grow to the extent that your future becomes *now* in reality almost instantaneously. Just by thinking coherent thoughts in a directed way, your thoughts will beam out like laser magic, achieving great results. This is a powerful and positive way to live your life because success and happiness then become self-maintaining.

For the past five years in over fifty centers around the world, the Global Consciousness Project (GCP) has been recording, on a network of devices sensitive to human mental and emotional frequencies, the variations and fluctuations that occur when large numbers of people are focused on the same event, such as 9/11. We already know that variations in this fluctuating force occur when large groups of people are focused on world events—disasters, celebrations, or other events that stir human thoughts and feelings. The GCP wants to learn about the global presence or consciousness. The project's research scientists are based at Princeton University in the United States and in other parts of the world (such as Britain and Germany). Dr. Roger Nelson, the director of the Global Consciousness Project at Princeton, says that in his opinion humans don't just stop at their skin. He believes that global consciousness is much bigger than the physical body, and reports that science has good evidence that there's an interaction between consciousness and physical systems.

World peace may be much nearer than we realize because, when global consciousness reaches critical mass, freedom is near. We have invented televisions and radios that pick up pictures and sounds in real time, when the signal is clearly transmitted. Your brain is so much more powerful than technology; it's a quantum device, able to transcend time and space.

An amazing experiment took place in 1993. Four thousand people meditated on peace for seven weeks in Washington, DC. The study was monitored by sociologists and criminologists from leading universities and representatives from the police and government departments. Variables such as weather, daylight hours, and time of year were taken into account. The results were astounding: violent crime and assaults went down by as much as 23 percent in the final week of the project, when the size of the group was largest. The statistical probability that this could reflect chance variation in crime levels is less than two in a billion.

The more connected and congruent your conscious and unconscious mind, the more easily your thoughts will resonate through the vibrational energy all around you. Whoever is on the same vibration will then be able to pick up on your thoughts as quickly as you think them! Thought "manipulation" will not work, by the way, because manipulation is a middle-brain mechanism of low-energy intent and therefore would set up an interference pattern, producing inconsistent results.

An interesting and thrilling development happened when I had been switching my language and my life for about eighteen months, with amazing success. I began waking up every morning with a sense of excitement and empowerment. People would telephone me or email me almost as soon as I formulated a thought, with solutions to my questions and people's names to contact, without any conversation having taken place! I found that my low-energy emotions appeared and cleared like a child's: flashes of emotion followed by feeling great in minutes, not in hours or days as before.

I truly realized that changing our language is something we can all do to produce profound results. This was demonstrated to me when my husband's sister Ann came to stay with us for two weeks. As we drove home from the airport she talked about how "hard" the journey was. She said the flight was "not bad," although the airline staff were very helpful. I could see Katie out of the corner of my eye wanting to speak to Ann, and motioned to her not to say anything since Ann didn't know about clearing or switching her language. In fact, we slipped right back into using low-energy words that we hadn't used for months!

For the next few days we explained to Ann why we speak differently and say "switch" to each other. Then we carried on as usual, using high-energy words and language. The second week of her visit, Will and I took time off work, and we spent a lot of time together as a family. That was when I suddenly realized that Ann was using high-energy language perfectly. There was not one low-energy word in her vocabulary! I know she's bright, but there was no way that she could have learned it that quickly. Then I remembered Sheldrake's morphic field theory, which states that when one person learns something, the information can be transferred to the rest of humanity in the same instant using the unique hidden variable at the level of the quantum field.

I remembered that I'd seen this once before and had been amazed by it then as well. Jade, our black standard poodle, had ten puppies. One of the puppies was determined to climb over the plastic safety gate. She tried every day for three weeks. None of the other puppies were interested; they were playing with each other, or looking for food or love.

One day she did it. The gate was two feet high, and she managed to climb over by using the holes in the pattern of the gate to lever herself out. It took less than ten seconds for every puppy to be over the same gate. This is Sheldrake's theory in action. I am always in awe of how instantaneously the information channel opens up when the intent is strong. It is clear that the power of focused intent can make a difference between succeeding and not succeeding.

For your own inner peace and contentment, you might want to record the following script and listen to it every day. The more you hear it, the more you will begin to loosen up your model of the world, making it easier for your natural state of joy to emerge. It's good to listen to it at night just before sleep, or in the morning just after awakening, as your inner and outer minds are more aligned at these times.

Fast-Forward to an Optimistic Future

(The full script is available on CD from my website: *www.Yvonne Oswald.com.*)

Perhaps you can allow yourself to close your eyes and . . . relax. You're breathing more deeply and more slowly . . . feel a beautiful, all-encompassing light, which flows through your body with every breath you take.

Imagine yourself on the shoulder of the most majestic mountain. There's a light breeze playing with your hair and the air smells fresh and clear. As you settle down now you may become aware of the sound of water bubbling from a nearby spring. You know that it will taste delicious.

The view from here is endless . . . as you look at the far horizon you can see fields and valleys, green trees and a beautiful blue sky. . . . There's a soft morning mist that falls damp against your skin. As the sun gets higher, fe . . . e . . . e . . . l the warmth enter your whole body and . . . just . . . let . . . go.

Absorb the sunlight through every pore, cell, organ, and tissue of your lovely body . . . now or in the next few minutes. You can feel the warmth enter your face, neck, and shoulders like liquid light, softening and releasing.

As the light moves over and through your heart, lungs, liver, and stomach, feel every cell heal and relax. The light goes through your hips to your legs, down through your knees and calves and into your feet, where you may feel a tingling as the sun renews every cell in your physical body with a healthy and new vitality.

As your awareness expands, take in the feeling of safety that this wonderful space in nature brings to you. Now find the most safe, sacred place that you have in your physical body, and just take your attention to that area. Or just imagine where that would be if you needed to choose a place. Feel the light and warmth flow into that area, and imagine a swirling vortex of energy spreading outward from the safe source. As you allow the light to expand, you may feel that the power of the energy is increasing.

You are expanding your awareness to the scene around you, to the mountaintop and sky . . . and you may recognize that you are a part of that light; in fact you are that soft, safe, all-encompassing light. You can do anything. . . . You can be anything you want to be. . . . You can be rich, happy, healthy, and successful if you . . . give yourself permission now.

Your unconscious mind is in touch with everything and everyone you need to know, and ready to bring you great opportunities to have a dynamic, compelling future. In fact, it's already experienced that wonderful future, because it has the ability to observe as though seeing it from the top of a mountain.

You can now accept and let go what cannot be changed and change what can be changed immediately as you awake. You may feel your chin lift and your shoulders release as you . . . realize *how well you are doing. You are now at a crossroads, and you know that there is only one path to take ... the one that is marked: Optimism and Action! You were born with an optimistic nature ... with a thirst for knowledge ... even before you had conscious awareness.*

Imagine yourself expanding your awareness to a place just above your physical body, then observe a river of time leading back into the past. Find yourself relaxing as you become part of this lovely scene, a scene as old as time itself. You learned many lessons as you traveled along this river—some of them perhaps not to your liking, some of them thrilling and exciting. All of these experiences are now part of your unconscious mind, giving you vast amounts of innate knowledge about life itself, allowing you to ... create new behavior patterns ... now.

Observe a shaft of sunlight shining down onto the river like a spotlight ... far, far back into the past ... back to the source of all light and life. Travel back into the source, back to the oneness. Watch and feel and listen as the river lights up with the glory (of God). Reflecting on the past, you are carrying the glinting light as it flows back to the present, dazzling and clearing any or all darker or dull memories as it returns to the present: the gift that is you today. Releasing all negative emotions and limiting decisions as you retain the positive lessons for future use—now.

As you finally feel the warmth of the sun, float back down into your physical body

Searching for solutions will become part of the excitement for you as you use the resources and skills that are second nature to you because you have reconnected with the beginning.

Your body, mind, and spirit are synchronizing, harmonizing, and integrating as you listen ... and your inner voice is telling you now that ... you are perfect. Every small change that you notice will reinforce the belief that the work you are doing is paying off physically, emotionally, and financially.

As you awaken you may become aware of a deep feeling of satisfaction: a security and a certainty that you are already on the path of change.

With every breath you take you are discovering wonderful things about yourself and with every discovery you are experiencing a deeper and more profound sense of satisfaction with your life.

You awake every morning feeling the best you've ever felt . . . amazed at how easy it is to . . . retain everything you are learning . . . healthy, free, wonderfully refreshed, and excited about your bright, compelling future, where you are rich, happy, healthy, and loving it. . . .

As I count backwards from five, you may find an amazing sense of joy inside you as you open your eyes.

Five . . . feeling that life is worth living with passion and power.

Four . . . loving the new you.

Three . . . more aware of your feet, legs, body and arms.

Two . . . becoming clear-headed and fully conscious.

And as you see, hear, or feel the number one in your head in the next thirty seconds, only when you are truly committed to being happy, open your eyes and feel great.

What Happens After You Live Happily Ever After?

You are now near the end of this book, but at the beginning of the excitement; you already know there's always more to explore! To plan future happiness, your final destination needs just a little further thought. Last year I taught a Magic of the Mind seminar at the Ontario Science Centre. I wanted to stretch people's minds beyond where their thoughts usually stopped. The forty or so people got into groups and each group was given the title of a fairy tale: "Cinderella," "Snow White," "Beauty and the Beast," "Sleeping Beauty," or "Hansel and Gretel."

The groups were given pieces of paper, each with the name of one of the characters from the story. This was done at random, because I soon realized that everyone wanted to be the character that had the happiest ending. Every character then had to explain to the others why they behaved as they did. So, for instance, the queen in "Snow White" explained that her childhood had been one of deprivation. My assistants and I listened as the excuses started flying—it actually became hilarious. The others in the group were encouraged to ask questions: for instance, to Snow White: "Why didn't you run away?"

I had asked them originally to resolve the exercise with a happy ending for everybody, but every single group ended with the original ending of the fairy story, "And then they lived happily ever after." I sent them back into groups and then asked them to stretch to get everyone a happy ending, including the not so nice characters. I also asked them to think about what happened after Cinderella got married. What did the prince do? When they really thought about it, they came up with some very interesting answers. "Cinderella" went like this:

Cinderella: After she had two children, a boy and a girl, she went on to open shelters for abused women and children.

The prince: He was a fair ruler. He started training people in fitness. He started a foundation for orphans because he was aware of what his wife had gone through.

The two sisters: Cinderella forgave them and found husbands for them both. One was very artistic, so she studied art and design to make homes beautiful. The other became a therapist after she had gone through three years of therapy herself.

The mother: She went to rehab (she had been a drinker), and then after five years of therapy, she traveled and married again, finding true love at last.

What are you planning for your own happy ending?

Imagine being at your eighty-fifth birthday party. People are talking about you and saying how great you are. Who is at your party? What do they say you're best at doing? What do you still want to do? What lasting impression have you made on other people's lives? What do you still do at eighty-five to keep you fit and active? (Make sure you start doing that now.) What work do you still love to do?

Close your eyes for a moment and imagine that scene. Imagine that you are talking to your eighty-five-year-old self. Ask this self what he or she wants you to be, do, or have right now to be happy and healthy at eighty-five. Then promise that fit, happy, fulfilled person that you'll make it easy for them, starting right now.

Speech Magic—Transform Your Life Using the Language of Success

Life is not measured by the number of breaths we take but by the moments that take our breath away.
—Author unknown

Like the parable of the seeds falling on fertile ground, we owe it to our children to nurture our language, our communication, and our actions. It's time. Begin doing this by living for today. Act as though you are rich, happy, healthy, loved, and special. Because you are. You are unique. You have skills and talents that no one else in the world has. You are so amazing. I believe that it's time now to create your thoughts to create your life. Awaken your senses; connect with your own abilities, potentials, and inner wisdom.

Words and thoughts have vibration and power beyond your wildest dreams. As you clear the old patterns of low-energy thoughts, low-energy words, low-energy actions, and unsupportive beliefs, you make connections with the power of light and life, and can manifest everything you ever want or need. An absence of light acts as a separation or disconnection from the source, which is the place where all abundance is accessible. Unencumbered thoughts radiate out and illuminate the darkness.

Whether you believe in God, quantum physics, both, or neither, the unifying force for humanity is that light is life-affirming, and the absence of light is non life affirming. It's time to shine out your light to bring the gift of awareness to everyone by teaching and passing on everything you have learned. It's time for kindness to everyone, including yourself and the planet. It's time for generosity of heart and mind. It's time for confidence and hope. We are strong when we're together.

The present is the only time we have to change the future.

You began reading this book thinking that you might learn something; in truth you were simply remembering what you already knew. You may remember the distance you have already traveled to come to this point in your journey. You are not traveling alone. You are part of the great oneness of life. You are not *looking* for knowledge or truth—you *are* knowledge, love, and truth.

When awareness and consciousness come together, you must then know that you can never end—you are perfect.

You always were.
Shine out your light.
Here's to Your Happiness.

A Message from Yvonne

I have been working with people for more than twenty-five years now. My focus has been to inspire them and help them create their own tools to succeed in life. I remember being with my spirit guide Peter during one of my early meditations. I was in a small cabin in a valley making a chair out of white cane. I knew that I had more to make.

"How many more do I need to do?" I asked. Each chair seemed to take me a long time.

"Look out of the window," he said. I gasped as I saw what seemed to be thousands of partially made chairs extending in a line as far as the eye could see.

"I'll never do all those!"

"One at a time," said Peter. "One at a time."

Many years later I was with a client who had a lot of work ahead of her to get her life back on track. I used this story to explain to her that the tasks she undertook to accomplish this had to be bite-sized. I suddenly realized that we were sitting in the exact same cane chairs that I had made at the cabin—and that since then I had helped make many thousands of people's lives happier by facilitating their sense of self-worth and belonging.

I had a similar experience when I began studying hypnotherapy. Peter and I were standing near the ocean. The breeze was fresh and the sun was shining. The sky was a crystal clear blue.

"What am I going to do with this new direction?" I asked.

"You're going to help all those people." He gestured toward the long stretch of seemingly endless beach, where there were people crowded together as far as I could see.

"No way!" I exclaimed. "That's too much for one person."

"Exactly," my guide said with a smile. "Let me show you how."

He offered me a lit candle with which to light the one I suddenly found in my hand. As I lit my candle from his, I noticed four women and a man in front of me. Each was holding a candle in one hand and extending it toward me.

I lit the five candles with mine, and they each turned and lit someone else's. I watched in awe as the whole beach was illuminated in a wave expanding into the distance. It was magical to see all the radiant, smiling faces as the light was passed along.

"Now *that* I can do," I said with relief.

I now pass the candlelight to you, knowing that you will feel just as honored as I have when you help people find the light and magic inside themselves.

Appendix

Switch These Low-Energy Phrases to High-Energy Phrases

No problem . . . . _____

Don't worry about it . . . . . . _____

I'm sick . . . . _____

Not bad . . . . _____

I'm starving . . . . _____

How depressing . . . . _____

It's too hard . . . . _____

I'm trying . . . . _____

It's a miserable drive . . . . _____

I'm afraid not . . . . _____

It's too expensive . . . . _____

I'm a bit broke right now . . . _____

A car accident . . . . _____

I hate cold weather . . . . _____

I have a headache . . . . _____

I'm sorry, I can't . . . . _____

Poor thing . . . . _____

What a shame . . . . _____

That's a nasty cut . . . . _____

I'm going on a diet . . . . _____

That's disgusting . . . . _____

I'm nervous . . . . _____

That hurts . . . . _____

That's annoying . . . . _____

Top Optimistic, High-Energy Words

Achieve
Baby
Beautiful
Believe
Choose/choice
Dream
Easy
Energy
Enthusiasm
Family
Father
Feel
Free
Funny
Future
God
Happy
Harmony
Heart
Humor
Improve

Knowledge
Mom
Money
New
Please
Popular
Positive
Present
Profit
Release
Results
Safety
Sexy
Smart
Success
Sweet
Thanks
Top
Unique
Value

Low-Energy Words to Clear from Your Language

Afraid
Angry
Anxiety
Bad
Blocked
Bottom
Broke
Cheap
Cheat
Control
Criticize
Dark
Difficult
Disease
Disempower
Doubt
Down
Envy

Expensive
Failure
Fear
Forget
Guilt
Hard
Hate
Idiot
Ill
Lazy
Lose/Loser
Mean
Nasty
Old
Poor
Problem
Put down
Rage

Reaction
Reduce
Rule
Sad
Separate
Shame
Sick
Small
Sorrow
Stupid
Sue
Trying
War
Weak
Worry
Worse

Ho'oponopono Adaptation

Release and Forgiveness—Open up Your Heart

Record the following script in your own voice and listen to it every day until you feel revitalized and enjoy a wonderful feeling of freedom. You'll be empowered with the results.

 The more you breathe, the more you relax. Imagine now, a magical forest, a beautiful safe place in nature. It's a lovely day. The trees are dappled in sunlight, the birds are singing sweetly, and you can hear the sound of water trickling over the rocks and pebbles from a nearby stream. You may smell cedar, pine, or damp earth.

Find a comfortable place in a clearing at the base of a strong oak tree. Sit down and just experience this feeling of tranquility and harmony, as you absorb all the knowledge and wisdom . . . from this great tree of the forest.

You . . . feel a sense of peace and safety in the dappled sunlight. Perhaps you can hear the leaves rustle as they play with the breeze. They seem to be giving you a message from your unconscious . . . mind to . . . just let go. Your conscious mind can listen now or simply continue observing the sounds and sights of nature.

You may observe the wooden bridge that is over the water. Raise your eyes to the bluest of blue skies . . . a sky that seems to go on forever. . . . Take a deep breath and allow yourself to let go . . . o . . . o . . . o . . . now. A shaft of sunlight slowly relaxes your whole body. As the cells, nerves, tissues, and organs absorb this wonderful light, breathe deeply and slowly, relaxing further with every breath. The sunlight makes its way automatically over your scalp, calming and softening your face, neck, and shoulders.

Take a deep breath and, as you release it, allow your shoulders to simply respond to gravity, absorbing the warming energy, easily releasing. The light moves down your spine, strengthening and clearing as it goes, rippling and relaxing. Feel a new suppleness in the muscles and nerves surrounding every vertebra.

As the warm, powerful, compelling light flows down though your body, feel every organ—your heart, liver, lungs, stomach—relax and free itself, moving in perfect harmony with the rest of the body.

Your arms and hands relax as the light enters every cell, renewing and revitalizing as it goes. You may feel a tingling sensation in your right or left hand—whichever hand this is for you—which simply shows you that you are relaxing even further. Your buttocks, hips, and genitals relax as the light moves downward over and through your body. You may notice a sensation of heaviness in your thighs, knees, and calves as you relax even further.

In this comfortable place of safety, you suddenly notice a wonderful angel standing to your left, who holds a laser of light. Observe the angel's presence of unconditional love, and allow yourself to be bathed in the golden glow of acceptance.

Now imagine some people standing across the other side of the bridge, in a circular area surrounded by trees. These are all the people you know this lifetime who have an emotional tie to you. You may see people there whom you haven't thought of in years.

Observe a person coming toward you over the bridge, and walk forward to meet this person . . . in the center of your clearing. Who is it? Notice that the person looks a little different from the way you remember because this is the person's higher self, dressed in flowing, beautiful robes.

You suddenly feel a cord attaching this person to your body. Where is the cord attached to you? (pause) . . . Where is the cord attached to their body? . . . (pause) Listen to this person asking your forgiveness for whatever he or she did to you, knowingly or unknowingly, in this lifetime or any other. As you sense that the life they lived was not easy, do you understand now why that person behaved the way he or she did? Can you feel softened?

It's now time to ask her or him for forgiveness for whatever you did, knowingly or unknowingly, this lifetime or any other.

When you have both come now to an understanding, ask the angel to clear the cord with the laser of light. Take a deep breath, hold it and . . . get ready to release . . . the breath . . . by saying the word "Now!" aloud when . . . you are ready (pause).

As the laser clears the cord, take a deep breath and feel the sensations of release and empowerment. Watch the cord turn into pure light and be reabsorbed by both yourself and the other person.

Feel how much stronger you are now. Observe the other person smiling at you gratefully, and stand a little taller. Watch as he or she leaves the clearing, goes back over the bridge with a spring in his or her step, and disappears into the forest.

You'll notice a group of people coming toward you from the other side of the bridge, excitedly smiling with anticipation at the thought of approaching freedom. As they gather in the . . . clearing before you, the path is open to new ways and endless possibilities for the future.

Notice the cords attaching you to the group and the group to you. You may see a number of cords attached to different parts of your body. How thick or thin are the cords?

Listen to all these people ask your forgiveness for whatever they did to you, knowingly or unknowingly, this lifetime or any other. As you sense that the life they lived was not easy, do you . . . understand now . . . why they behaved the way they did? Can you . . . feel softened by the knowledge . . . ? It's time now to ask their forgiveness for whatever you did, knowingly or unknowingly, in this lifetime or any other.

When you have come to an understanding, ask the angel to clear the cords with the laser of light. Take a deep breath, hold it, and . . . get ready to release . . . the breath . . . by saying the word "Now!" aloud when . . . you are ready (pause).

As the laser clears the cord, breathe a deep breath . . . feel the sensation of release and empowerment. Watch the cords turn into the pure light of joy and be reabsorbed by both yourself and the people, into the heart center.

Feel how much stronger you are now. Observe everyone smiling at you gratefully and stand a little taller. Watch as they leave the clearing and go back over the bridge with a spring in their step. They are laughing, waving, and talking as they disappear into the forest.

The angel puts down the laser of light and embraces you. Feel the approval and unconditional love of the angel, take a deep breath, and become aware of a new sensation of lightness in your body.

It's a feeling that you know you accept and forgive others. You know that you forgive and accept yourself, fully and completely now.

Representational System Predicates

Visual	Auditory	Kinesthetic	Auditory-Digital
Appear	Announce	Brush	Analyze
Brilliant	Articulate	Caress	Balance
Clean-looking	Audible	Catch my drift	Be conscious of
Clear	Be all ears	Catch on	Call to mind
Colorful	Converse	Explore	Come to mind
Envision	Deaf	Feel	Comprehend
Focus	Declare	Firm hold	Consider
Glance	Harmony	Get a grasp	Convincing
Illuminate	Hear	Get hold of	Decide
Imagine	Intone	Get in touch	Evaluate
Lay eyes on	In tune with	Get the hang of	Informed
Light	Listen	Gut/funny feeling	Judge
Look	Loud	Heated	Know
Lucid	Make music	Inhale	Learn about
Magnify	Noisy	Make contact	Logical
Notice	Outspoken	Reach out	Make sense of
Picture	Quiet	Sense	Plan
Point of view	Resonant	Smell	Process
Reveal	Silent	Smooth	Question
See	Soft	Sticky	Remember
Symbolic	Speak	Stroke	Scan
View	Talk	Taste	Sort out
Visible	Tell	Tender	Study
Visualize	Tune in/out	Touch base	Think
Vivid	Verbalize	Warm	Understand

Further Reading

Ball, Pamela. *10,000 Dreams Interpreted*. New York: Gramercy, 2000.

Bandler, Richard. *Using Your Brain—for a Change*. Boulder, CO: Real People Press, 1985.

Birdwhistle, Raymond. *Kinetics and Context*. Philadelphia: University of Pennsylvania Press, 1970.

Buffett, Mary, and David Clark. *Buffettology*. New York: Scribner, 1999.

Burroughs, Stanley. *The Master Cleanser*. Reno, NV: Burroughs Books, 1993.

Byrne, Rhonda. *The Secret*. New York: Atria Books/Beyond Words, 2006.

Chamberlain, David. *Babies Remember Birth*. New York: Ballantine, 1989.

Chopra, Deepak. *Perfect Health*. New York: Harmony, 1991.

———. *Quantum Healing*. New York: Bantam, 1989.

Clark, Hulda Regehr. *The Cure for All Diseases*. San Diego: Pro Perkins, 1995.

Covey, Stephen. *The 7 Habits of Highly Effective People*. New York: Fireside, 1990.

Doulis, Alex. *Take Your Money and Run.* Toronto: Uphill Publishing, 1998.

Eker, T. Harv. *Secrets of the Millionaire Mind.* New York: HarperCollins, 2005.

Emoto, Masaru. *Love Thyself.* Carlsbad, CA: Hay House, 2004.

Hawkins, David. *Power vs. Force.* Carlsbad, CA: Hay House, 2002.

Hay, Louise. *You Can Heal Your Life.* Santa Monica, CA: Hay House, 1987.

Hill, Napoleon. *Napoleon Hill's Keys to Success.* New York: Dutton, 1994.

———. *Think and Grow Rich.* San Diego: Aventine Press, rev. ed., 2004.

Isles, Greg. *The Footprints of God.* New York: Pocket Star, 2004.

James, Tad. *The Secret of Creating Your Future.* Honolulu: Profit-Ability Group, 1989.

Kiyosaki, Robert T. *Rich Dad's Retire Young, Retire Rich.* New York: Warner, 2002.

———. *Rich Dad, Poor Dad.* New York: Warner Business, 2000.

Labay, Mary Lee, and Kevin Hogan. *Through the Open Door: Secrets of Self-Hypnosis.* Gretna, LA: Pelican, 2000.

Lewis, Byron, and Frank Pucelik. *Magic of NLP Demystified.* Portland, OR: Metamorphous Press, 1990.

Lundahl, Craig R., and Harold A. Widdison. *The Eternal Journey.* New York: Warner Books, 1997.

McTaggart, Lynne. *The Field.* New York: HarperCollins, 2002.

Murphy, Joseph. *Your Infinite Power to Be Rich.* New York: Prentice-Hall, 1968.

Orman, Suze. *The Laws of Money, the Lessons of Life*. New York: Free Press, 2005.

Roberts, Ken. *A Rich Man's Secret*. St. Paul, MN: Llewellyn Publications, 1995.

Sobel, Milo. *The 12-Hour MBA Program*. Englewood Cliffs, NJ: Prentice-Hall, 1994.

Ty, Brother. *God Is My Broker*. New York: Fireside, 1995.

Urban, Hal. *Positive Words, Powerful Results*. New York: Fireside, 2004.

Vernay, Thomas, and John Kelly. *The Secret Life of the Unborn Child*. New York: Summit, 1981.

Whitney, Russ. *Building Wealth*. New York: Fireside, 1995.